WORCESTER
1651

Worcester 1651

Malcolm Atkin

Pen & Sword

First published in Great Britain in 2008 by
Pen & Sword Military
an imprint of
Pen & Sword Books Ltd
47 Church Street
Barnsley
South Yorkshire
S70 2AS

ISBN 978-1-84415-080-9

A CIP catalogue record for this book is available from the British Library

Typeset in 10/11.5pt Palatino by
Mac Style, Nafferton, E. Yorkshire

Printed and bound in the UK by
CPI

Pen & Sword Books Ltd incorporates the Imprints of Pen & Sword
Aviation, Pen & Sword Maritime, Pen & Sword Military, Wharncliffe
Local History, Pen and Sword Select, Pen and Sword Military Classics
and Leo Cooper.

For a complete list of Pen & Sword titles please contact
PEN & SWORD BOOKS LIMITED
47 Church Street, Barnsley, South Yorkshire, S70 2AS, England
E-mail: enquiries@pen-and-sword.co.uk
Website: www.pen-and-sword.co.uk

CONTENTS

PREFACE

Say you have been at Worcester, where England's sorrows began, and where they are happily ended.[1]

The battle of Worcester on 3 September 1651 had great significance as the final battle of the Civil Wars. The soldiers there realised that they were taking part in a piece of history – rushing so as not to miss the fight and subsequently exhorted by Cromwell's chaplain to tell their wives and children where they had been. The wars of 1642–51 are still generally referred to as the 'English' Civil Wars, although they affected Scotland, Wales and Ireland as much as England and as a consequence are sometimes alternatively called the 'Wars of the Three Kingdoms'. By 1651 the struggle had clearly become a national conflict between Scotland and England, with the Scottish army perceived as a foreign invader rather than a supporter of their lawful King. Victory was therefore seen as a national triumph.

The battle cannot be regarded as the isolated action of a single day. It was the culmination of a campaign that began with Cromwell enticing Charles II to invade England. Thereafter, the fate of the Scottish army rested in the hands of a shepherding Parliamentary army until overwhelming forces could be brought to bear to completely destroy the Royalist threat. The present work develops the argument first proposed by the pioneering Worcester historian J.W. Willis-Bund, in 1905, that the battle as it unfolded on 3 September was largely an accident. Cromwell's initial plan may have been only to encircle the city in preparation for a siege, but his ability to plan the campaign on a countrywide basis, to move large bodies of troops across an 8-mile front on the battlefield and finally to take immediate advantage of opportunities that arose remains a testimony to his military skill. If the outcome of the campaign was inevitable then the manner of the Royalist defeat was not.

Although the battle is usually seen as a triumph of Cromwell's New Model Army (England's first standing army), the present book also describes the key role of the part-time militias, drawn from all across the country. They had come a long way from the much-derided Trained Bands of 1642 and their participation in large numbers is a testimony to the popular enthusiasm in England for the campaign. In particular, the militia dragoon regiments played a key role, at a time when the regular New Model Army dragoons were being converted to Horse.

The Civil Wars were as horrific as any images of modern civil wars that we see on our television screens. One should cast aside the Victorian romanticism which still persists in elements of the modern imagination. The reality was very different, as best expressed in the surviving letters of those who took part: defeat at Worcester was a national disaster for Scotland. The battlefield was not an abstract concept as is sometimes suggested by neatly drawn plans of troop dispositions. This book also considers the impact of the battle on the local population, both in the initial recruiting for the armies and their supply, and then in the 'mopping up' operations.

For a battle in which English opinion was remarkably united it might seem strange that popular attention has tended to focus on the romantic appeal of the Scots. What would local people 350 years ago have thought of a memorial to the Scottish dead as now constructed at Powick? Fortunately the passage of time allows us to acknowledge the sacrifices that both sides made for their beliefs. One hundred years ago Willis-Bund bemoaned the fact that 'the last, the greatest, the fiercest fight of all is unmarked, unhonoured, and unknown', recounting the story of the historian who was directed to the site of an early nineteenth-century boxing match as the only 'battle' that the local guide could think of! Today there is still no interpretation on the major surviving monument of Fort Royal and in 2006 the toposcope overlooking the Severn/Teme crossing is derelict. It is hoped that the City Council and the newly formed Battle of Worcester Society, can improve the degree of on-site interpretation of the battlefield and raise the awareness of the battle beyond the simple, and inaccurate, marketing slogan of Worcester as the 'faithful city'. But perhaps the best memorial after all is the coincidence that the modern civic war memorial outside the Cathedral does actually lie on the documented place where so many of the casualties of the battle were buried. Unknowingly perhaps, every year Worcester remembers the dead not just of modern times but also from those dramatic days when Worcester was itself a battleground.

Chapter One

The Campaign in Scotland, 1650

They were look'd upon rather as flying than as marching into England; and few Men will put themselves into a flying army which is pursued by the conquering enemy.[1]

The battle of Worcester on 3 September 1651 was the final act of a series of Civil Wars between King and Parliament that had begun in August 1642 and led to the execution of the monarch, Charles I, in January 1649. In an accident of fate, both the first and last battles of this tumultuous period in British history were to take place in Worcester.[2] By the time of the final phase of this conflict (the Third Civil War, 1650–1), however, it had become less of a civil war and more of a national conflict between England and Scotland.

The reasons for originally going to war had been a complex mix of national politics and religion, fuelled by more local disputes. Charles I was accused of pursuing a path that would give power to Roman Catholics and for exercising what some now saw as an outdated belief, promoted by his father James I, that he could rule absolutely through the divine right of majesty. His opponents in a neglected Parliament chafed at their lack of influence as the King raised taxes without their consent and waged war in Ireland and Scotland. Only the lack of money to fund the wars had obliged Charles to recall Parliament in 1640 after an eleven-year absence. But this demand for a share in government by the King's subjects was in turn seen as presumptuous. Parliament was dominated by sects that feared the High Church predilections of Charles I (encouraged by his Roman Catholic wife, Queen Henrietta Maria). It was feared that the Laudian reforms of the Church were merely a stepping-stone towards an attempt to return the country to Roman Catholicism as the state religion, perhaps even enforced through the presence of an Irish army – leading to a return to the religious persecutions of the Tudor period. Instead, many in Parliament favoured the Presbyterian system of a more devolved system of Church government. Independents were to go further during the course of the struggle and deny any need for a Church hierarchy at all. 'No Bishops, No Popery' became a popular slogan in the Parliamentary army. In Scotland, power was in the hands of the Covenanters, who were supporters of the

Scottish National Covenant of 1638 which had been drawn up to resist any further change in religious practice in Scotland. There were also economic divisions in the country with the trading and manufacturing classes, especially in the towns, generally supporting Parliament against the monopolist policies of the Crown.

The Royalists were defeated at the end of the First Civil War in 1646: Worcester was the last English city in their hands to fall, although it could not be claimed to be a 'Royalist' city but rather a place that had been under Royalist occupation for three and a half years. Indeed, there had been a great deal of sympathy in Worcester before the war towards the Parliamentary cause.[3] The Second Civil War of 1648–9 saw a realignment of forces as disenchanted Parliamentarians and Presbyterians supported the imprisoned Charles I against the rising influence of the Independents and the army high command. The latter increasingly saw themselves as representing the true interests of the people against a self-serving Parliament. Worcester took no part in the Royalist risings. Significantly, the Scots now changed sides, in return for an assurance from the King that he would support their version of Presbyterianism in England. The Scottish army was, however, defeated and the sporadic revolts were all suppressed. The machinations of the King in building an alliance with their former ally convinced the army and its supporters in Parliament that attempts to negotiate with him were hopeless, and in January 1649 Charles, that 'Man of Blood', was tried and executed.

By the tradition of royal succession, the 18-year-old Charles, Prince of Wales (1630–85), then in exile in the Hague, automatically became King upon the death of his father. The Covenanters in Scotland formally proclaimed him as sovereign a few days later and the new Charles II became the centre of new intrigue by his courtiers. Encouraged by letters protesting their continuing support from English Royalists, Charles's entourage convinced him that the country was simply waiting for him to return before rising in support of the monarchy. They were heartened in their beliefs by the civilian population's continuing dislike of the high costs of the new standing army and by divisions within the New Model Army itself, as evidenced by the rise of the Leveller movement during 1647 and its violent suppression in 1649. By August 1651, with 21,000 men in Scotland, England's first professional army was costing over £2 million per annum.[4]

Charles had the choice of using either Ireland or Scotland as his base to reconquer his kingdom. But an army under Oliver Cromwell (still only second-in-command of the Parliamentary army) had been dispatched to Ireland in August 1649 and by May 1650 the country had been ruthlessly

CHARLES II (1630–85)

The eldest son of King Charles I (executed in January 1649) and his French Queen, Henrietta Maria, the young prince had been obliged to grow up quickly. Aged just 12, he had been at Edgehill, where at one point he had to hide in a barn full of wounded soldiers. In February 1644, in order to become a figurehead around which to rally support, he was made the nominal General of the Midlands Association. In November 1644 the 14-year-old was given the title 'first Captain-General of all our Forces', although real command was in the hands of Prince Rupert. By the end of the First Civil War Prince Charles had retreated to Cornwall, where he rashly decided to attack Fairfax's army near Truro. His troops were defeated and he was forced to flee the country. Although his military experience was largely nominal, he took personal command during the battle of Worcester. This was probably the only way to coordinate his squabbling generals. Although no doubt part-propaganda, all the Royalist accounts pay tribute to his personal bravery in the battle and the manner in which he had repeatedly tried to rally his forces. He may have deliberately tried to cultivate a 'common touch', and despite his later reputation for flamboyance, during the campaign he dressed simply in back- and breastplate over a buff coat, with grey breeches. In part this may have been a matter of necessity within the poverty-stricken army. He was reported to have only changed his shirt twice during the march south.

Charles II. (By courtesy of Worcester City Library)

The Worcester campaign and the subsequent drama of his escape may be taken as one of the episodes of which Charles was most proud. Certainly he never tired of recounting his adventures as a fugitive. Although he later had a reputation for duplicity, he remained fiercely loyal to those who had played a genuine part in his escape, and was equally dismissive of those who tried to capitalise on the story. His generosity did not extend to the Scottish army that had loyally followed him to what was widely seen as an inevitable defeat. He never forgave the Scots for the treatment he had received when he landed in Scotland in 1650 and galled them by later complaining that they had not fought well enough, an accusation for which a number of clans never forgave the Stuarts.

CHRONOLOGY OF THE THIRD CIVIL WAR

1649

30 January	Execution of Charles I
5 February	Charles II proclaimed King in Scotland
17 March	Abolition of the monarchy

1650

24 June	Charles II lands in Scotland
26 June	Fairfax resigns commission in favour of Cromwell
22 July	Parliamentary army enters Scotland
16 August	Charles II forced to sign Declaration of his father's responsibility for the wars
3 September	Battle of Dunbar (defeat of Covenanter army)
30 November	Defeat of western Covenanters at Hamilton
24 December	Surrender of Edinburgh Castle to Cromwell

1651

1 January	Charles II crowned in Scotland
17 April	Campaign in Scotland renewed
20 July	Battle of Inverkeithing (Parliamentary victory)
1 August	Charles II and the Scottish army enter England; Cromwell at Perth
9 August	Scottish army enters Carlisle
14 August	Parliamentary troops under Lambert and Harrison rendezvous at Haslemoor to shadow Scottish army; Cromwell at Newcastle
16 August	Skirmish at Warrington; Cromwell at Catterick
17 August	Earl of Derby's rendezvous with Scottish army
22 August	Scottish army enters Worcester; Cromwell at Rufford Abbey, Nottinghamshire
24 August	Cromwell's rendezvous with Lambert and Harrison at Warwick
25 August	Battle of Wigan (Parliamentary victory); Scottish outpost established at Upton-upon-Severn
26 August	Abortive muster on Pitchcroft, Worcester; Cromwell at Stratford-upon-Avon
27 August	Cromwell's army of 28,000 men gathers at Evesham
28 August	Lambert captures bridge at Upton-upon-Severn
29 August	Parliamentary army occupies high ground on east side of Worcester
31 August	Earl of Derby enters Worcester with survivors from the battle of Wigan
3 September	Battle of Worcester

'pacified' and neutralised as a Royalist base. The Scottish alternative was to be uncomfortable from the start. When the Earl of Argyll and the Covenanters proclaimed Charles II as King in Scotland on 5 February 1649, they made it clear that the exercise of royal powers was dependent on him signing the Covenant. With this conditional support behind him, the young King Charles II, aged only 20, landed at Garmouth-on-Spey (north of Aberdeen) in Scotland on 24 June 1650. But it was not a happy homecoming. His Scottish Covenanter allies, wishing to retain the purity of their cause, refused to accept an alliance with High Church and Catholic Royalists. Indeed, the butchered remains of Charles's former Captain-General in Scotland, James Graham, Marquis of Montrose (1612–50), were still impaled above the gates of Aberdeen and Dundee following the failure of his Royalist rising against the Covenanters of March 1650 and subsequent execution in May. Charles had disassociated himself from Montrose, abandoning him to his gruesome fate of being hanged, drawn and quartered, in order to secure the alliance with the Covenanters. One might, however, wonder as to the King's thoughts as he rode through the city gate of Aberdeen over which still hung a dismembered arm of his devoted Scottish supporter. The Covenanters placed the young Charles under what amounted to house arrest in Dunfermline until he signed the Covenant for the establishment of Presbyterianism as the official religion in England. He was subjected to repeated, seemingly endless, sermons and was obliged to declare that his father had been to blame for the First Civil War, and that his mother, Henrietta Maria, was a French idolatress. Following this effort at religious brainwashing, at his coronation on 1 January 1651 he was left to bemoan that 'I think I must repent too that ever I was born'. The alliance divided Scottish opinion. The Scots were not all the automatic Stuart supporters of later legend and many shared in the distrust of the late Charles I and now his son. Covenanters distrusted Engagers (those who had tried to make an alliance with Charles I in return for a promise only temporarily to establish Presbyterianism in England); Lowlander distrusted Highlander; and the Highland clans distrusted one another! The alliance also distanced the King from his more natural supporters among the English High Church and the Catholics.

Amid such tensions, the Royalist Thomas Lord Bruce spoke disdainfully of the 'mongrel Scotch army' and the newsletter *Mercurius Politicus* dismissed the alliance of Cavalier and Presbyterian as coming together under the 'disguise of the Covenant'.[5] The continuing rift between the English and Scottish allies was to blight the coming campaign. In a move that was unlikely to have improved relations, a sham fight between the English and Scottish troops was arranged in the Royalist camp on 29 May

1651 to celebrate the King's birthday. The English general, Edward Massie, routed the Scots, exuberantly driving them off the field in what he claimed was only a jest – but it angered his now-humiliated allies.[6] When the army eventually moved into England George Villiers, Duke of Buckingham (1627–87), a childhood friend of Charles, claimed the right to lead the army, as the most senior English nobleman present. He had been appointed General of the Royalist Eastern Association in May 1650, despite his relative military inexperience. Now aged 23, he had fought as a mere 15-year-old at Lichfield in 1643 and had then taken part in the revolts of the Second Civil War. This was hardly comparable to the experience of the other battle-hardened Thirty Years War and First Civil War veterans in the army, such as the Scottish Leslie or English Massie. Worse, Buckingham had a reputation for being quarrelsome and reckless; when his demands were refused he sulked and refused to attend council meetings, talk to the King, or even change his clothes. It is hardly a surprise in such rancorous circumstances that the young King Charles took personal charge of the campaign 'all absolutely under the command of his Majesty' as the only means of creating some semblance of unity within his divided army.[7]

With Charles back in his kingdom, the leaders of the new Commonwealth (established 'by the supreme authority of this nation, the representatives of the People in Parliament . . . and that without any King or House of Lords') were also divided as to how to react to the new threat. The commander-in-chief of the Parliamentary army was General 'Black Tom' Fairfax (1612–71), himself a veteran of the Thirty Years War and chosen to command the professional New Model Army created in 1645. He refused to invade the homeland of his former Scottish ally and resigned his command as Lord General in favour of his second-in-command, the now more famous Oliver Cromwell (1599–1658), who was recalled from service in Ireland for the task. Previously the respected and feared commander of the Horse under Fairfax, Cromwell was a much more astute politician than his commander-in-chief. Indeed, he was a rare combination of soldier and politician, driven above all by his religious belief, and ready to resist any attempt to further divide the country in a new civil war.

In June 1650 Cromwell marched a 16,000-strong army into Scotland but it was not to be a happy campaign. Apart from the resignation of Fairfax, Cromwell found it difficult to recruit other experienced officers. The Kidderminster preacher Richard Baxter (a former Parliamentary army chaplain) refused to pray for the success of the war. He wrote to the soldiers in Scotland 'to help them understand what a crime it was to force men to pray for the success of those that were violating their covenant and loyalty, and going in such a cause to kill their bretheren'.[8] None of this

OLIVER CROMWELL (1599–1658)

Oliver Cromwell.

Oliver Cromwell is perhaps the most famous figure to emerge from the Civil War period, although it was only in the Third Civil War from 1650 that he assumed complete command of the Parliamentary army. The battle of Worcester was the last time that he personally took part on the field of battle.

A Huntingdonshire yeoman, he became an MP in the late 1620s and then rose to prominence as a vocal critic of Charles I's government. He was driven by his religious beliefs and although this might on occasion mean that he would delay a decision until he was convinced that he was following God's commands, he would then act decisively, if not ruthlessly. Although he had no previous military experience, he soon won a reputation as a skilful cavalry commander in Lincolnshire and was made a lieutenant-general in 1644. Cromwell played a decisive role in the Marston Moor campaign, alongside his enemy-to-be at Worcester, David Leslie. In 1645 he became second-in-command of the new unified Parliamentary army – the New Model Army – under Sir Thomas Fairfax. Despite the 'Self-Denying Ordinance' which was supposed to separate political and military power, he remained an MP, although siding with the army in the ultimately futile negotiations with Charles I. Having lost patience with the King's machinations, Cromwell was one of the prime movers behind the King's trial and execution. But he was not a revolutionary as such – in order to protect the unity of the army he also suppressed the burgeoning democratic movement of the Levellers. In 1649–50 he was on campaign in Ireland, including the now-infamous storming of Drogheda and the massacre of its garrison (although the scale of civilian deaths has been questioned). Cromwell returned to take overall command of the New Model Army on the resignation of Fairfax in June 1650. Having defeated Charles II in Worcester he became Lord Protector in 1653 but refused the crown. He died on 3 September 1658 and the republic survived less than another two years. Legend had it that he sold his soul to the Devil in return for victory at Worcester and when he died a nationwide storm – 'Oliver's Wind' – marked the Devil claiming his own! He was not, however, left to lie in peace and following the Restoration his body was exhumed and dismembered. As a consequence, one of the most famous Englishmen has no burial place.

could have helped morale. David Leslie (1601–82), Cromwell's former ally from the battle of Marston Moor, fought a skilful campaign. The Parliamentary army, wracked by disease and outnumbered, was pushed back to the sea port of Dunbar, following a failed attempt to seize control of the road to Stirling and then bring the Scots to a decisive battle. The English troops were cut off and defeat must have seemed inevitable for what was described as a 'poor, shattered, hungry, discouraged army' of now only 11,000 'sound men'.[9] Seizing the initiative, although heavily outnumbered, Cromwell launched a pre-emptive strike at dawn on 3 September and surprised the Scots in their tents. In a lesson that was not to be learned by the time of Worcester, many of the Scottish officers had retired to shelter away from their units and confusion raged. Some 3,000 Scots were reported killed and another 10,000 captured by the New Model Army. According to Cromwell, the Scots were 'made by the Lord of Hosts as stubble to our swords'. Many of the prisoners were sent as indentured servants, virtual slaves, to the New World – an ominous precedent for what happened after the battle of Worcester a year later.

The opportunity for a quick, decisive victory for the Royalist cause was lost at Dunbar. If the New Model Army had been severely mauled or captured in Scotland, then hesitant Royalist supporters in England may well have found the courage to rise and the course of history could have been very different. However, far from being distraught by his defeat, Charles was reported to have danced at the news that the dour Covenanter army had been decimated and seized this as an opportunity to at last introduce 'malignant' (i.e. non-Covenanter) Royalists into his army. At least any final victory might then be more on his own terms than those of the Covenanters. Whether true or not, the contemporary account of his joy at the Covenanter discomfort can again hardly have helped unite the King's forces. Leslie's defensive line had been broken and the Scottish capital of Edinburgh and the port of Leith fell to Cromwell. Leslie withdrew to Stirling. However, despite the Scots having lost almost half their army, Dunbar equally failed to give Cromwell a decisive victory and the war continued into the winter. The Scottish weather took its toll, and the English army became again wracked with dysentery. Edinburgh housewives were obliged to give up their sheets to make tents for the cold and wet army. Cromwell himself suffered a bout of his recurrent malaria (a common illness in his native East Anglian fens during this period). After Dunbar the weary 51-year-old had written home to his wife in exhaustion, 'I grow an old man, and feel infirmities of age marvellously stealing upon me'.[10] He was indeed old by the standards of his contemporary general officers. During the Worcester campaign the average age of the generals was only in the early 30s. Problems continued into the spring, with complaints over lack of pay and an increasing amount of desertion. With Leslie trying to avoid coming to battle, Cromwell determined that his army could not risk a second winter campaign in Scotland. He did not recover his own health fully until June 1651, by which time he was planning to engineer events so as to bring the campaign back into England and to a battleground more of his choosing.

In a move that gives a foretaste of the tactics used in the battle of Worcester, Cromwell successfully wrong-footed the Scottish army and, while enemy attention was focused on diversionary skirmishing in the west, Major-General John Lambert (1619–84), the commissary-general, crossed the Firth of Forth. This was evidently an operation planned well in advance, with flatboats brought up for the purpose to ferry Lambert's men across the Forth. With the Parliamentary army now operating on two fronts, Leslie was undecided as to which force to attack, and on 20 July 1651 Lambert routed the Scots at Inverkeithing, Fife, killing around 2,000 of the enemy and taking another 1,400 prisoner. With the breadbasket of Fife captured, Perth was taken on 2 August in order to cut Charles off from any further support from the Highlands. At the same time the Parliamentary army was also reorganised in preparation for what was recognised as the final decisive campaign. Inferior officers were weeded out and discipline was tightened. Cromwell chose his officers not only for their ability but also for their religious fervour. As a consequence the army that was to seek the final battle against the Scots was both experienced and united in purpose, convinced that it was on a divine mission.

Having cut the Scots off from the prospect of any resupply from the north, Cromwell's strategy now was to tempt the enemy into England in a bid to capture the capital. In so doing, he would try to draw the Scots out into open battle at a place and time when they could be destroyed by overwhelming strength. Cromwell calculated that not only would they lengthen their supply line from their base in Scotland, but that this act of invasion by an army that few on either side in England had much cause to welcome would unite the country against the hated enemy. England had been exhausted by two civil wars and now most people, whatever their initial allegiances, simply prayed for time to recover and rebuild their lives and livelihoods. Already in January 1651 Cromwell had written to the Council of State to set the scene by saying that the Scots now 'make it not a religious war, but a national quarrel'.[11] In the face of actual invasion, Cromwell wrote to Parliament on 4 August to reassure them and explain that although Charles's march into England 'will trouble some men's thoughts, and may occasion some inconveniences, of which I hope we are as deeply sensible, and have, and I trust shall be, as dilligent to prevent as any'. The alternative would be 'another winter's warre, to the ruine of your soldiery'.[12] Cromwell was assisted by a sympathetic press, with *Mercurius Politicus* in August obligingly publishing a history of Scottish invasions of England since 1071, suggesting that any Englishman who was so

WILLIAM, 2ND DUKE OF HAMILTON (1616–51)

William, Duke of Hamilton, was one of Charles II's generals at the battle of Worcester, with some accounts describing him as commander of the Scottish forces. He succeeded to the dukedom after his brother's execution in 1649, following the defeat of the latter at Preston in the preceding year. William had been arrested by Charles I at Oxford in 1643 and tried to negotiate with him on behalf of the Scots in 1646 to persuade him to accept Presbyterianism. However, in 1647 he signed, on behalf of the Scots, the 'Engagement' treaty with Charles at Carisbrooke Castle. Under the terms of this

The Duke of Hamilton. (By courtesy of Worcester City Library)

agreement, a Scottish army would invade England on behalf of the King, in return for which Charles promised to impose Presbyterianism in England for a period of three years and to suppress the Independent sects. In addition, Scots were to be given a greater influence in the government of England leading to eventual union of the two kingdoms. But because Charles did not personally agree to take the Covenant, extreme Presbyterians, including David Leslie, refused to support the Engager army. After the failure of the Second Civil War Hamilton fled to Holland, returning to Scotland with Charles II in 1650. He was mortally wounded in the battle of Worcester, while leading one arm of the Royalist counter-attack on Perry Wood. He is buried in Worcester Cathedral.

DAVID LESLIE (1601–82)

David Leslie was the commander of the Scottish Horse during the battle of Worcester. He was born in Fife, the son of the 1st Earl of Lindores. He served as a colonel of cavalry in the large Scottish contingent fighting on behalf of King Gustav Adolfus of Sweden in the Thirty Years War, but returned in 1640 to fight for Scotland in the Bishops' Wars. In July 1644, fighting on the side of Parliament in the army of the Covenant, he took part in the battle of Marston Moor as second-in-command of the Scottish army under his uncle, Alexander Leslie, Earl of Levan. Ironically in view of later events, at Marston Moor he commanded a brigade of Scottish Horse under Oliver Cromwell. In 1645 he routed the Marquis of Montrose

David Leslie.

(later to become Charles II's Captain General in Scotland) at Philiphaugh and then reduced a number of the Scottish clans that had supported the Royalists. In 1647, however, he became Lieutenant General of the Scottish Covenanter army, now ready to invade England to rescue the King from English army hands (although he later refused to support the Engagers). In 1650 he was the commanding officer of the army that ultimately captured Montrose, who was then executed. In these confusing times Leslie then joined the Covenanter alliance with Charles II when he landed. He became the effective commander of Charles II's army in Scotland, under the titular command still of the Earl of Levan. At Worcester, after Charles had taken personal control of the army, Leslie commanded the Scottish cavalry but refused to engage them with the enemy, leading to accusations of cowardice (which his subsequent elevation to the peerage would seem to disprove). After his capture he was imprisoned in the Tower of London where he turned to drink. He remained there until the Restoration in 1660, when he was released and granted the title of Baron Newark. He died in 1682.

unpatriotic as to join the Scots should be stoned as a traitor! The plan was to work better than he could have ever hoped for and the campaign of 1651 is notable for a rare sense of popular enthusiasm for the Civil Wars and support for the new Commonwealth.

With the main Parliamentary army to the north in Perth, cutting off the Scottish supply route from the Highlands, the prospect of an unopposed entry into England was too tempting for King Charles. As a consequence, nudged into action by Cromwell, on 31 July the King left Stirling for England with an army of some 7,000–9,000 Foot and 3,000–4,000 Horse (estimates of numbers vary). According to Fleetwood, most of the Foot were Highlanders.[13] Some of the men were accompanied by their wives (as attested by the subsequent need to find prisoners 'without wives' for work on the fen drainage scheme). Although his courtiers may still have dreamed of a mass Royalist uprising in England, Charles's more realistic Scottish generals knew that this was a dangerous gamble, splitting their forces (as an army had to remain in Scotland to face the troops left by Cromwell under General Monck). Hamilton described the invasion as 'a desperate venture in which people were laughing at the ridiculousness of our condition'. For Hamilton, the greatest argument for invasion was simple: 'I cannot tell you whether our hopes or fears are greatest: but we have one stout argument, despair.'[14] In his words, the alternatives were either to starve or to disband. Richard Baxter echoed these feelings, regarding Charles's march into England as being more a sign of his defeat in retreating from Cromwell than an advance to reclaim his throne: 'The success of Cromwell at Dunbarre and afterwards had put a Fear upon all Men, and the manner of the Scots, coming away, persuaded all Men that Necessity forced them, and they were look'd upon rather as flying than as marching into England; and few Men will put themselves into a flying army which is pursued by the conquering enemy.'[15] Many of the extreme Covenanters had regarded the repeated defeats to their cause in 1650–1 as a sign of divine disapproval of their alliance with Charles II. The Covenanter leader, the Earl of Argyll, was one notable figure who now refused to support the Royalist cause any further. The Duke of Hamilton wrote from Penrith on 8 August that 'All the rogues have left us. I will not say whether for fear or disloyalty.' Leslie, now commander of the Scottish Horse, went into a deep depression from which he never recovered. He believed (prophetically as far as his own cavalry was concerned) that the army, 'how soever it looked, would not fight'. With such an attitude at the level of the high command, it is hardly surprising that many men refused to march into England at all and other troops deserted en route. At Nantwich Charles had to go 'cap in hand' to his troops to persuade them

Scottish leather cannon. (By courtesy of the Royal Armouries)

to continue.[16] It seems probable that Charles was once again swayed by his English courtiers. The latter had repeatedly claimed that thousands in England were eagerly awaiting his arrival before rising up against the Commonwealth but none such materialised. Charles later berated his Scottish troops for their failure to give him a victory, but the very fact that an army followed him into England at all in such circumstances is a testimony to their simple loyalty to the King.

As Cromwell had anticipated, panic did ensue in some Parliamentary quarters at this turn of events: 'Some could not hide very pale and unmanly fears, and were in such distraction of spirit, that it much disturbed their councils.'[17] The Scots entered England on 1 August but they were given little room to manoeuvre in their invasion, and must soon have realised that they were being funnelled into a dangerous trap. Leaving Monck in command in Scotland, Cromwell brought about 10,000 men of the New Model Army down the east side of the country from Perth. They comprised nine regiments of Foot, two regiments of Horse and the light artillery. Unlike the Scots, the English could count on immediate reinforcements to their army, with a national mobilisation of the militias having been ordered in May 1651. That from Worcester mustered on

20

22 May.[18] The fanatical Fifth Monarchist and regicide Major-General Thomas Harrison (1606–60), who had been left in England to command the army while Cromwell was in Scotland, mobilised a militia army of over 3,000 Horse and Dragoons of the northern militias from Berwick southwards, together with newly raised regiments of the New Model Army. The county militia were the successors of the pre-Civil War Trained Bands. In 1642, with some notable exceptions, they were considered of little value. The principal problems had been their lack of training and their unwillingness to serve outside their county boundary. They were either disbanded and their arms used elsewhere or the men were transferred into new regiments of 'volunteers' that were less parochial in their constitution. But the Third Civil War saw a resurgence of their role, with the militia ranks now swelled by battle-hardened veterans and stiffened with officers transferred from the professional regiments of the New Model Army. Both Harrison and Cromwell had expressed concerns about the likely contribution of the militias but they played a key role throughout the campaign, especially at the battle of Worcester itself. Here, as an added precaution, the regiments of militia were brigaded with regiments of the New Model Army to provide additional stiffening.

The main force of the New Model Army was kept out of immediate contact with the Scots but moved down the east side of the country to intercept them further to the south. Meanwhile, Harrison moved westwards from Newcastle with his militias in order to box in the Scottish advance and prevent any break-out towards London. To improve mobility, two companies of Nottinghamshire Foot were quickly converted to Dragoons. Their instructions were to 'flank them [the Scots], straighten their provisions, and do service as you can see opportunities upon them'.[19] One such skirmish was at Appleby, where a force of up to 12 troops of Harrison's Horse (about 700 men) engaged and then fell back from the Scots, encouraging them further into the country. At the same time Lambert held 4,000 crack New Model Horse behind the Scottish army, blocking the escape route of the latter back to Scotland. Lambert and Harrison rendezvoused on Haslemoor, Lancashire (north of Bolton), on 14 August with a combined strength of 12,000–14,000 men. This was already approximately equal to the size of the Scottish army. Around 3,000 men were reported to have joined the Parliamentary army from Lancashire. This contrasts sharply with the failure of the Royalists to recruit from the same area. Further afield, General Charles Fleetwood (Cromwell's former second-in-command in Scotland until February 1651 and now a member of the Council of State) was organising the raising of the militias in the Midlands to protect the capital. In London itself General Philip Skippon (d. 1660) commanded another 15,000 men. Skippon's own military experience dated back to 1622 when he had served in Vere's English Brigade during the Thirty Years War. He was idolised by his men and respected by his enemies. The capital was in solid, capable hands. Another 5,000 men were mobilised from Wales and the south-west, rendezvousing in Gloucester, under the command of its governor, Sir William Constable (1582–1655), another Independent regicide. These troops would act as the final backstop to the Scottish advance. As an added precaution, the navy under General Blake also patrolled the North Sea against any possible move to reinforce the Royalists from France. He had already destroyed a Royalist privateer fleet in November 1650. The scale of mobilisation is clear evidence that this was a campaign organised in depth across the whole country. Nothing was being left to chance in this 'snare that God hath laid for them'.[20]

Parliament also fought a very effective intelligence war. Potential supporters of the King were arrested or at least prevented from moving freely; commissions of martial law were issued to officers to discourage any revolt. In the Isle of Ely Parliamentary *agents provocateurs* had actually encouraged a former Royalist officer, Eusabius Andrews, to plan a rebellion. Once exposed, the Royalist sympathisers were arrested and in August 1650 Andrews was executed. In January 1651 another Parliamentary agent managed to acquire letters that gave a breakdown of Royalist organisation in England. Further potential supporters were rounded up following the arrest in March 1651 of a Royalist agent, Thomas Coke, who promptly informed against his contacts, including London merchants who had promised financial support. The Royalist organisation was in complete disarray. In Worcester the prison under the Tolsey and the Crown Inn on Broad Street was used to imprison local suspected Royalists. Others, such as the former Royalist commander Samuel Sandys, were prevented from returning to the county (Sandys was held in Oxford from May). The defences of a number of towns, including Worcester, were also ordered to be levelled in the spring of 1651, in order to hinder any attempt at rebellion, although there is no specific evidence to suggest that the Royalists had particularly targeted Worcestershire as a possible focus for rebellion. Its inhabitants had taken little part in the Second Civil War. In June, under the misapprehension that the King had already invaded and was within 40 miles of them, around 400 Cardigan Royalists did rise. The reaction of the local Parliamentary forces was swift: 40 of the Royalists were killed, 60 taken prisoner and the rest dispersed. This was a clear lesson for any others considering open action.

Despite some fears from the Council of State, the strategy worked exactly as Cromwell had hoped. Thousands of men obeyed a new call to join the local militias in defence against the foreign invader. Fairfax put aside his former concerns and raised 2,400 men of the Yorkshire militia to join the national mobilisation. The militias then marched to final rendezvous points at St Albans, Northampton, Oxford and Gloucester. Those arriving in Northampton included militias from Leicestershire, Rutland, Warwickshire, Oxfordshire, Bedfordshire, Huntingdonshire and Buckinghamshire as well as Northamptonshire itself. The country had become a huge chess-board on which Cromwell was carefully placing his pieces for the final military check-mate. Given the perennial complaints in the army about long-standing arrears of pay and the traditional reluctance of the militia to serve outside their own counties, the Council of State also took the precaution of ensuring that the militia were well paid. County Committees were ordered to find one month's wages for the men in advance. One week's pay was to be paid immediately with the balance held back until they reached the various rendezvous points. That at least was the theory: the Cheshire Militia were, however, still claiming that two months' pay (£1,218) remained outstanding in December 1656.[21]

As the Scottish army marched south it found little support. With the recent experience of the Cardiganshire Royalists in mind, few were prepared to make a stand against the hardened troops of the New Model Army or, indeed, risk exposure to Cromwell's intelligence system. The principal mobiliser of English support was to be 44-year-old James Stanley, the Earl of Derby (1607–51), who landed in Lancashire from the Isle of Man, to where he had fled in 1644. But he was able only to recruit a miserly 1,500 men to the cause from his home base in Lancashire. Significantly he could only manage this after the Scots had passed by, so reluctant were the local Royalists to be seen to be associating with them. Not for the first or last time, the King's Covenanter allies seemed to pursue a self-defeating attitude. The dour Committee of Ministers travelling with the army circulated a declaration after the army entered England expressing concern that Charles was not fully committed to the Covenant and forbidding him to 'receive or entertain any soldiers in his troops, but those that would subscribe that obligation'.[22] Charles wrote to Massie, who was leading the advance guard into England, telling him to ignore any such declaration – but it had already been well circulated. To make matters worse, agents of the Council of State also intercepted the letter of 18 August from Charles to Massie and it was gleefully published to demonstrate the divisions in the Royalist ranks.[23] The Scots were also short of food and supplies. On 7 August Harrison had ordered that horses, cattle and provisions should be removed from ahead of their line of march so as to deny succour to the Scots. Charles was desperate to improve the reputation of his men (described by Harrison as caterpillars that devoured the land!) and tried to forbid any looting by his desperate soldiers. Some men were reported to have been executed for stealing apples and one man was executed simply for taking a pint of beer without paying for it.[24] Such examples may only have been token gestures and seemed to have little effect; the Scots were again accused of looting the countryside. In Cumberland they were accused of destroying mills, and in Cheshire the Horse were reported to have eaten whole fields of corn.[25] Charles could not keep his starving army in check for long. Whitelock claimed that 'after passing Warrington the Scots began to plunder extremely, and many of them were weak'.[26] Whether such stories were merely propaganda or not, by the time they reached Nantwich they were described as being 'discontented and sick', with dysentery spreading through the ranks. By 19 August Massie was complaining that his horses were exhausted.

By contrast, a coordinated effort by the Council of State in London and Cromwell on his line of march mounted a highly efficient logistics operation. Daily messages were dispatched to and fro at a feverish pace to arrange food and replacement mounts as the army moved south at a rate of 20 miles per day. The pace was such that Cromwell allowed his men to march in their shirt sleeves – in a period when the shirt was considered to be part of a man's underwear. The regicide Thomas Scott and a former mayor of Worcester, Richard Salway, were used as couriers to ride between

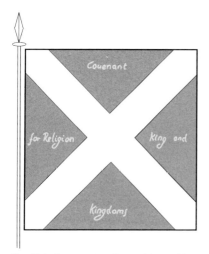

Scottish Covenanter flag, with a white cross and lettering on a blue ground.

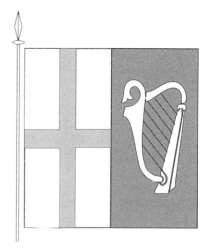

The Commonwealth flag of the English forces, with a red St George's cross and a gold Irish harp on a blue field.

the Council of State and the army. As well as organisation, the Parliamentary forces had the great advantage over their Scottish opponents that they could pay cash for supplies. On 18 August Cromwell wrote from Ripon to the Mayor and Corporation of Doncaster advising them that he would be requiring bread, cheese, butter and meat to be supplied when his army arrived but that 'the country shall receive ready money'.[27] By 26 August the artillery train had worn out their draught horses and a hundred more animals had to be commandeered from Northamptonshire at a cost of £300 18s 2d.[28] Other orders were sent to gather materials for the final battle. Once the Scots entered Worcester a siege was clearly expected and on 26 August Cromwell ordered 'five thousand shovels, spades and pickaxes, thirty tons of match and four hundred barrels of gunpowder' to be sent to Gloucester, ready to be moved up to the army at its final rendezvous.[29] Even with such support, the speed of the march – covering 300 miles in three weeks with only one day's rest – left many exhausted. Some of the sick had to be left behind to recover on the route of march from Northumberland into Leicestershire. Some of Harrison's men may have been left at Northfield (near Birmingham).

Cromwell was content to allow the Scots to continue to move south, keeping his main army at a safe distance and thereby avoiding any decisive engagement until he was ready. There was a small skirmish on 16 August with a reported 9,000 of Lambert's men at the crossing over the River Mersey at Warrington. Lambert, however, refused to be drawn into a major engagement. The local commander, the Baptist and regicide Robert Lilburne (1635–65), continued to harry the Scots with minor skirmishes while the enemy passed through his territory and then, despite being outnumbered, delivered a crushing defeat against the Earl of Derby's new English forces still trying to recruit in the area. Lilburne's Regiment of Horse and the garrisons of Chester and Liverpool engaged Derby's troops at Wigan on 25 August, killed 60 of the Royalists and took another 400 men prisoner. There was little more that Derby could do but flee southwards and limp into Worcester with his surviving men. They were not a good advert for joining the Royalist cause!

Chapter Two

The Net Tightens

Some small pickerings there was and poppings of musqueteers behind the hedges but nothing considerable was attempted.[1]

Colonel Robert Stapleton

As the Scots continued south, the evidence suggests that Cromwell was expecting finally to confront the Scots at loyalist Gloucester, where 5,000 troops were waiting as a backstop. One of the Royalist leaders was Edward Massie (*c.* 1619–74), Parliamentary hero of Gloucester in the First Civil War but now second-in-command (under Buckingham) of the Royalist English troops. Massie had optimistically promised to raise local support from Gloucestershire, presumably on the basis of a supposed continuing personal loyalty to their former commander. Instead, the citizens of Gloucester rushed to join the new Parliamentary militia, with 700 men reported as joining in just two days. Depression continued to mount in the Royalist ranks when they reached Shrewsbury, where the resolute Colonel Mackworth refused to allow them shelter in the town. Disconsolately they marched onwards through Staffordshire to Wolverhampton.

In Worcestershire the Council of State had in March 1651 promoted a militia officer, Colonel John James of Astley, to be garrison commander of Worcester with orders to raise and command the Horse and Dragoons of the Worcestershire militia.[2] One of his problems (a common complaint throughout the Civil Wars) had been to find sufficient mounts for his men. On the day following a muster of levied troops on 22 May he had to return some horses supplied by Gloucester as being 'of stature too little and quality so bad'.[3] To add to his problems, some of his men had also been taken in May and June for regular service in the New Model Army. These may have included the four men pressed from Northfield parish on 22 May and 24 June at a total cost of £6 3s.[4] None the less, once the Scots crossed the River Stour into the county near Kidderminster, the Worcestershire militia under Colonel James and Captain Andrew Yarranton, like Lilburne's men before them, fought a running engagement to slow down the advance of the Scots and win more time for Cromwell's armies to complete their rendezvous. The Worcestershire men were supported by a levy of militia Horse from Gloucester, no doubt eager to delay any battle on their own doorstep.[5]

With the Scottish army getting closer, the earlier instructions of the Council of State to make Worcester untenable were countermanded and the defences of Worcester were now ordered to be rebuilt. If the Council of State had some earlier concerns about the loyalties of Worcester (repeatedly during March and April sending reminders for the defences to be levelled), these fears had now been satisfied. On 15 August the Council of State wrote to the Militia Commissioners of the county congratulating them over the 'good posture' of the county. Contrary to the later legend of the 'loyal and faithful city', the citizens claimed they did 'hazard our lives in the keeping of the City and did what we could to strengthen the walls, and the well-affected in the City and County came in to us willingly engaging themselves'.[6] Gates were blocked with banks of earth, derelict walls patched and defence ditches cleaned out. On 19 August there was a general muster of the militia on Pitchcroft, just outside the city defences on the north side. The men included a contingent, including Horse, from the parish of Northfield, in what was then the far north of Worcestershire (now the outskirts of Birmingham), brought at a cost of £1 2s 6d.[7] By 21 August

There was a skirmish between the Scots and the Worcestershire Militia at Ombersley on 22 August as the Scots advanced towards Worcester.

the Scots were at Kidderminster and Yarranton attempted to demolish part of the bridge across the Severn at Bewdley in order to prevent any support for them coming from Wales. As they advanced through Hartlebury, 11 miles (17km) north of Worcester, the Worcestershire Dragoons – a mobile force of musketeers who rode into battle but then fought on foot – were said to have 'beat back the enemy several times'. Hartlebury parish had suffered particularly badly from the Scots in 1645, when their army had driven off most of the sheep and looted many of the houses. No one there was likely to be a friend to the advancing army.

But the small force of militia could not stem the tide of the Scottish advance for long. With the enemy almost at the city gates, the resolve of the City Council to resist the Scots in the same manner as Shrewsbury crumbled. Some of the citizens who had volunteered to join the militia decided to resign. After a heated debate during the evening of 21 August between the City Council, the County Committee and the militia officers, they agreed to surrender, probably hoping that the Scottish army would move on after a short rest. But the militia, now reinforced by five troops of Welsh Horse sent by Harrison, refused to give up and fought on during 22 August, with a further skirmish at Ombersley (just 5 miles from Worcester) and then fighting back to the walls of Worcester itself. In an action that outraged Parliament, the citizens signalled their new-found loyalty to the Crown by firing on their own men as the rearguard, under Captain Boyleston of Bewdley, removed the magazine of seven firkins of powder from the city and finally retreated to Gloucester. The advance guard of the Scots finally entered the city on the night of 22 August. The King waited outside at Whiteladies in Barbourne, in order to make a ceremonial entrance the next day at noon, probably through St Martin's Gate. Charles was greeted by the mayor, Thomas Lysons, and the sheriff, James Brydges, and was formally proclaimed 'King of Great Britain, France and Ireland'. Despite the pomp, the evidence of the fresh defence works would have been all around to show the King how the city had so recently been preparing to defend itself against him. At this stage Cromwell's army was in Nottinghamshire, preparing to link up with the militia from the Midlands.

Despite the hopes of the City Council, the Scots were too exhausted to travel any further. They had only had one day's rest (at Penrith) during their long march. Even King Charles had only managed to change his shirt twice during the whole journey. Most of the men camped inside Worcester, billeted on houses, inns, the Cathedral, Deanery and Guildhall. In addition, around 2,500 men may have been encamped in and around St John's. The parishioners of St Michael Bedwardine (the area from the

Bishop's Palace and Cathedral to the site of the castle) complained that they had borne one-tenth of the burden of housing the troops. At this time the population of Worcester was around 7,000 inhabitants, already suffering overcrowding owing to the destruction caused in the First Civil War. Even in normal circumstances the conditions were unsanitary by modern standards. One privy in the Trinity served twenty-four almshouses and the streets were frequently obstructed by 'muck hills'. Many families would have lived in a single room. Now the city had to feed and house thousands of troops. Any sanitary provision is likely to have completely collapsed. The 3,000-strong Scottish Horse under David Leslie were stationed on the flat open land at Pitchcroft to the north of the city defences. This was the traditional muster site of the local Trained Bands or militia. The Duke of Hamilton set up his HQ in the Wylde family home in Sidbury to cover the east and south sides of the city. A former medieval hospital known from the thirteenth century as the Commandery (owing to connections with the Knights Hospitallers), this building stood just outside the medieval defences and Sidbury Gate (on the site now occupied by the King's Head public house), but was protected by the recent eastward extension to the defences. Charles established his quarters between the two commands in what is now known as King Charles House on New Street, close to St Martin's Gate. At the time this was the town house of the Royalist Berkeley family. An observation post was also established on the tower of the Cathedral, with panoramic views of the surrounding area.

One of the Scottish officers was dismissive of the state of Worcester when they arrived as 'neither fortified nor victualled, only an old broken wall, and a fort, in a manner slighted'.[8] The hasty work of the Parliamentary garrison and citizens in repairing the Worcester defences was now continued under Scottish direction on a scale that was described as being 'beyond imagination'.[9] No time was lost. On Sunday 24 August, just a day after the main force entered the city, King Charles ordered the people of Salwarpe parish, near Droitwich, to 'send out of your parish 30 able men to work at the fortifications of this city, and in regard of the necessity to begin tomorrow morning (Monday) at 5 o'clock, whereof you and they are not to fail, as you tender our displeasure'.[10] The form of the defences is shown by the plan of 1660, depicting the layout at the battle of 1651. The basis of the defence was still the medieval walls and ditches, and seven fortified gates making an arc around the Severn river frontage. The medieval defences ran north from the bridge over the Severn (then between Tyebridge Street to the west and Newport Street, rather than on the site of the modern bridge) along the river bank, enclosing the church of

Photographic survey of part of the city wall, showing the patching of damage probably caused during the battle. (By courtesy of Worcestershire Historic Environment and Archaeology Service)

St Clement. They then turned east inside the line of The Butts and Sansome Street, interrupted by the gate on Foregate Street. The line of the wall and ditch then turned south on the line of the modern City Walls Road, with St Martin's Gate on the south side of the Cornmarket. It carried on (off the line of City Walls Road) to Sidbury Gate (now the King's Head public house). The line of the defences then turned to the west, enclosing the site of St Peter's church, and running along King Street before linking up with the mound of the former castle. It then followed the line of the quayside wall north along the riverbank back to Bridge Gate. The walls were 1.8m thick and by now had been lined with earth banks at least 2m wide, which were intended to dampen the impact of any cannon shot. The gates would be expected to be the focal point of any assault. By the start of the battle most had been blocked with earth piled into ground-floor rooms and by earth banks, or at least temporary wooden barricades, across the entries. In front of the walls were ditches up to 16m wide and part of the work on the defences entailed cleaning these out. In order to provide a clear route

around the walls for the defenders, outbuildings backing on to the defences were levelled or burned down.[11] Most of the suburbs had also been levelled by the Royalist garrison during the First Civil War so as to provide a clear field of fire. The major additions to the defences during the Civil War were extensions to the east, focused on Fort Royal, and a new defensive line beyond the site of the medieval castle and in front of Severn Street, which incorporated two triangular bastions.

Worcester lies in a bowl, with the River Severn to the west and an enclosing arc of high ground to the east. To protect the city from the latter a spur on to the higher ground had been built off the line of the existing medieval defences during the First Civil War, with a small fort at its outer point. The Scots rebuilt this on a massive scale as the star-shaped Fort Royal, described by a Parliamentary officer surveying the defences prior to the battle as 'a very fair and large fort'.[12] It both commanded the high ground of Red Hill and Green Hill, and protected the main east entrance to the city along what is now London Road (which originally ran further to

View from the tower of Worcester Cathedral, looking east towards Fort Royal and Red Hill.

the south of the fort). Fort Royal survives now only in a heavily landscaped form but the outline of two of the triangular corner bastions, designed to carry cannon, is still clear. Originally it would have been surrounded by a ditch, with the ramparts topped by a palisade. A late eighteenth-century plan also shows an outer line of defence just to the east, incorporating a diamond-shaped bastion, and with a ditch cutting across the line of London Road. There was also originally a covered way that provided a protected route off the high ground back to the Commandery. Although impressive, the works were, however, only half complete at the time of the battle. Men from the parish of Ripple had been summoned as forced labour to work on the defences. No doubt to their further irritation, six months after the battle they were recalled to help level the fort![13] South of the Cathedral the derelict castle on top of its motte was also refortified with a small star fort to carry cannon, as shown in the plan of 1660. Storm poles

driven into the sides of the mound were intended to hinder any assault.
The site of the castle has been completely destroyed, but it lay within the
loop of what is now Severn Street. Archaeological excavation has provided
graphic information on the scale of the defences at this time. Those on
Severn Street were 8–10m wide and 2.4m deep. On the north side of the
city, facing the line of the approaching Scots, the ditch excavated on The
Butts was over 16m wide and 3.5m deep. There is no evidence, however,
that the 10–16m wide, flat-bottomed, medieval ditch on the east side of the
city (City Walls Road) was cleaned out in the seventeenth century, the
defenders perhaps relying on the boggy nature of the ground in that part
of the city. By 1651 much of its line was also included within the protection
of the outer works extending to Fort Royal, with the ditch itself therefore
forming only a secondary line of defence.

The final element in the defensive network of the city was to clear the
suburbs of any buildings within musket range of the city walls. This

*Detail from an engraving of 1764, showing the remains of the castle mound to the
south of the Cathedral.*

View from the tower of Worcester Cathedral, looking north. The medieval bridge was between the present bridge and the railway viaduct. The Scottish Horse were camped on Pitchcroft, in the upper right of the picture (the modern racecourse).

continued a process begun from June 1643 (during the First Civil War) and was a clear reminder to the city of the new totality of war.[14] So complete was the clearance that after the war the Dean and Chapter, as one of the major landowners of Worcester, complained that they could no longer tell the boundaries of their properties. Displaced inhabitants would have added to the crush of people now crowded into Worcester.

On the west side of the Severn was the small hamlet of St John's. This was linked to Worcester via a medieval bridge lying 200m north of the present bridge (which dates to the late eighteenth century), at the end of Newport Street. The bridge was defended by a central tower with drawbridge and by a large triangular bastion built during the Civil Wars to cover the west approach. It was evidently an impressive piece of work, for Leland called the bridge 'a royal peace of work, highe and stronge', while Ogilby described it as 'a fair stone bridge with a tower thereon'.[15]

Nehemiah Wharton had described it in 1642 as 'a stronge stone bridge . . . consistinge of sixe arches, with a gate in the middle of the bridge, as strong as that on London Bridge, with a percullis'.[16] The standard practice at the time was to partly demolish bridges to prevent mass attack (as employed at Upton, Powick and Bransford), although here it was presumably thought that the drawbridge gave enough security.

St John's was reached from the bridge via a causeway (Tyebridge Street) across the flood meadows. There was a small cluster of houses beside this street, some of which were destroyed when the bastion in front of the bridge was built. Other buildings at the west end of the causeway in Cripplegate (where the land rises towards St John's) had already been destroyed during the siege of 1646. St John's itself was a small cluster of buildings, built around the triangular market in front of the church. Up to 2,500 men may have been quartered in St John's, ready to defend the west approaches to the city if the Teme were crossed. The local population would have been completely swamped by such numbers as their settlement was turned into an armed camp. But the Teme river frontage itself was only thinly garrisoned by some 600 Highlanders in brigades under Colonel Keith and Major-General Pitscottie, presumably because the river was thought (correctly as it turned out) to be an effective natural barrier. These men were to play a crucial role in the battle. On 25 August the Scots broke down part of the bridge at Powick and dug some form of entrenchments nearby. The latter probably took the form of a rudimentary fortified camp on Hobmore Hill (now the area of Columbia Drive), on a similar scale to the surviving works at Upton to protect the crossing. Only the bridge at Bransford was left intact at this stage, to allow the entry of support from Wales, or for a retreat westwards into Wales if necessary. Although the flat floodplain and land bounding it might initially seem to have been tempting ground for a classic open battle, the network of hedged fields was to prove difficult for manoeuvring large bodies of troops, especially the Horse.

On 25 August an outpost of 300 Dragoons and Horse was established 9 miles to the south at the crucial bridging point over the River Severn at Upton-upon-Severn, under the command of Edward Massie. Here they broke down one span of the bridge across the river (a few metres south of the present bridge), replacing it with a single plank for temporary passage. They also dug a rectangular earthwork to block the road back to Worcester (just beyond the present Severn Cottages). The purpose of the garrison was to guard against any advance of troops from Gloucester and protect a possible route of further advance southwards. But Massie established his own HQ a mile north of Upton, in the comfort of Hanley Castle, the home

EDWARD MASSIE (C. 1619–74)

Edward Massie was second-in-command of the English forces in the Worcester campaign and commanded the strategic outpost at Upton-upon-Severn. He was a professional soldier who had served on the continent in the Thirty Years War and had then been an engineer officer in the Bishops' Wars of 1639–40. At the start of the Civil War he had tried to get a commission in the Royalist army but then decided, according to Clarendon, that there were better prospects of promotion with Parliament and therefore went to London and was appointed a lieutenant colonel under the Earl of Stamford. He was made deputy governor of Gloucester in December 1642 and governor in the following year. He became a national Parliamentary hero for his successful defence of Gloucester during the siege of August–September 1643, winning a reputation for courage and for his clear tactical thinking. Thereafter Massie mounted a vigorous campaign to secure the county and even launched a raid into neighbouring Worcestershire. He captured Evesham in May 1645. But Massie had a great ego and fell out with the Gloucester politicians whom he accused of interference. His departure in June 1645 to become commander of the Western Association received a mixed reception from the Gloucestershire establishment. This fall from favour was to be important for the subsequent Worcester campaign. He became an MP in July 1646 but, as a Presbyterian in the power struggle between Parliament and the army, he gained the enmity of the Independent army command who described him as 'a profane man, unfit for command'. The next few years saw him flitting to and from the continent. He was impeached in June 1647 and fled to Holland. Although he returned in the following year, in January 1649 he once again had to escape to the continent where he offered his services to Charles II. He went with Charles to Scotland and fought at Inverkeithing before returning once again to the continent. He was back in Scotland in 1651 in time to join the Worcester campaign. His failure to ensure that there was a proper guard on the bridge at Upton-upon-Severn in the opening stages of the battle was to have momentous consequences, but he was severely wounded so that, according to Clarendon, 'he was in great torment, and could not stir out of his bed, in a time when his activity and industry was most useful'. Although captured, Massie's adventures continued: he escaped from the Tower of London and spent the next seven years travelling throughout England and the continent in a succession of abortive Royalist plots. After the Restoration he became MP for Gloucester and was then appointed Governor of Jamaica. He died in 1674.

General Edward Massie.

of the Parliamentarian Nicholas Lechmere at Severn End. Another 150 Scottish Horse were also quartered here. This division of forces and lack of direct supervision was a mistake that was possibly to prove fatal to the eventual outcome of the battle. Between the base at Upton and the Teme another small outpost was established at the moated manor house at Madresfield. Again this was owned by a Parliamentary family, the Lygons (who had been obliged to lay siege to their own property in the closing stages of the First Civil War).

Despite all these efforts, Clarendon later complained that the Scots failed to construct proper defences that took advantage of the lie of the land.[17] This is probably a reference to the way in which Worcester's defences were overlooked on the east side by the row of wooded hills (Red Hill, Perry Hill, etc.), guarded only by intermittent patrols, and to the absence of defences or significant garrisons beside the Teme (where the first attack was to fall). No doubt the Scots were encouraged by recent history when the Worcester defences (even before their improvements) and a small garrison of just 1,507 men had held off a substantial Parliamentary army for over six weeks.[18]

Having worked in partnership with Cromwell to agree the political scope of the campaign and ensure a smooth logistical operation, the Council of State formally passed over all responsibility for the campaign to Cromwell on 22 August. With the exhausted Scots ensconced within Worcester the die was cast and this now became a purely military operation. Cromwell ordered the final rendezvous of his field army for 27 August at the strategic river crossing of Evesham, 13 miles east of Worcester and commanding the route east from Worcester to London. This finally united the troops of Lambert, Fleetwood and Harrison with his own men. The outline of the campaign may already have been decided. Somewhat indiscreetly, on 27 August, even before the army was established at Evesham, the Council of State released a circular to the militia committees across the country informing them that the army was now 'come to a conjunction, and able to divide and attack the enemy on both sides of the Severn'.[19]

The two armies had probably reached Worcestershire in similar states of exhaustion – but the difference was that the Parliamentary army could now resupply itself at will and Cromwell could dictate the pace of events. Worcester was reported as being poorly 'victualled' at the entry of the Scots and it would have become increasingly difficult to bring in supplies as the Parliamentary army approached and began its own foraging. With the odds so stacked against them, it is not surprising that messengers sent out to Hereford, Gloucester and elsewhere failed to bring in any additional troops to the Royalist camp. Meanwhile, the fast-approaching Parliamentary army was re-equipping itself ready for the impending battle. Some of Harrison's Horse took remounts from Northfield parish as they entered Worcestershire. They included 'a sorell nag of Mr Byrch' worth £3 for one of Captain Lane's soldiers and a mare from William Smythe for a soldier under Captain Powell, worth £4 10s.[20] The County Committees of the neighbouring counties – Warwickshire, Gloucestershire, Shropshire and Herefordshire – were ordered to make ready supplies. With the hasty surrender of Worcester fresh in mind, a special note was left for the Worcestershire militia to gather together provisions 'and thereby show how little you approve of what your revolting city hath done'.[21]

An army of 30,000 men was now camped in and around Evesham. Finds of musket-balls and powder-flask tops suggest that part of the camp was on Greenhill to the north-east of the town but the troops must have been scattered over a large part of the Vale. Apart from the 20,000 or so men of the New Model Army, these included around 10,000 from the militias raised by Harrison and Fleetwood. Contingents are recorded from Essex, Suffolk, Cheshire, Northamptonshire, Oxfordshire, Surrey, Gloucestershire and Worcestershire itself. Those from Essex were reported to have run to ensure that they reached Worcester in time for the battle, arriving within only eleven days of first receiving their orders. This alone gives an indication of the enthusiasm to defeat the foreign enemy and the realisation that this was to be a momentous, historic confrontation. This was an event to overcome what had been widely perceived as an aversion to military service: something that would, in Whitelocke's words, make men 'leave a soft bed, close curtains and a warm chamber; to leave the choicest and most delicate fare of meats and wines for a little coarse bread and dirty water, with a foul pipe of tobacco; to leave the pleasing discourse and conversation of friends, wives and children for the dreadful whistling of bullets and bodies dropping dead at one's feet'.[22] The Surrey militia were less enthusiastic and some units of Foot were reported to have slowed their march until it was clear which side had won (although their Horse or Dragoons did take part in the battle). Together the New Model Army and the militia support were unwisely dismissed by Royalists as the 'scum and froth of the whole kingdom'.[23] But so confident did Cromwell feel that he countermanded orders for Lilburne's Lancashire militia to join the Evesham rendezvous, deploying them instead to cover any possible Scottish retreat. Behind Lilburne, Sir Arthur Haselrigg moved his men into position in Westmorland and Cumberland to 'utterly extirpate and destroy' any Scots that somehow managed to survive that far. So Cromwell's plan for the battle included not only the events on the

The Deanery, dating to 1730. Its predecessor was used as a billet for Royalist officers during the Scottish occupation of the city.

battlefield but also its likely aftermath. But with a note of caution, 5,000 militia were also held back in reserve at Coventry to protect the Midlands from any break-out eastwards.

Apart from a numerical superiority of nearly 2:1, Parliament had an overwhelming superiority in artillery. Cromwell brought down one train of artillery from Scotland and two further trains were dispatched from London. The field guns ranged from the easily portable robinet firing a $^3/_4$lb ball to the 9lb (4kg) demi-culverin with a range of about 1,800 paces. Cromwell had left his heavier siege cannon in Scotland but it is likely that some were included in the London artillery trains. The largest gun at the time was the cannon royal which fired a 63lb ball but no shot of this size has yet been recorded from Worcester. By contrast the Scots, under their General of Artillery James Wemyss of Caskierberran (1610–67), had brought only sixteen light leather cannon, limited to firing a cannon-ball of about $1^1/_2$lb or anti-personnel case-shot and not designed for protracted use. Built around the core of an iron tube, which was then bound in hemp and covered with a leather sleeve, they could be mounted singly, in pairs or even in fours. A cannon mounted singly could be drawn by just one horse. It is possible that a number of heavier cannon had been left in the city by the retreating Parliamentary garrison, although it might have been supposed that these had been 'spiked' to prevent their use. Critically, the ability of the Scots to resupply themselves with gunpowder would have been limited. They were reliant on what they had brought from Scotland, possibly the product from powder mills within Worcester (as existed in the First Civil War) and what was in the powder store in the corner of All Saints' churchyard beside Angel Lane. Lead was stripped from roofs (including the gatehouse of

THE ORGANISATION OF THE ARMIES AT WORCESTER

The armies of both sides were organised into regiments of three basic types of troops, Infantry, Horse and Dragoons, grouped on the battlefield into brigades. They tended to be known by the name of their commanding officer, although the New Model Army did have an official numbering system for its regiments.[24] In the field the regiments would often be commanded by the lieutenant-colonel and this explains the apparent confusion at Worcester where a number of titular colonels fought separately from the regiments that bore their name. The English infantry regiments of the time had a strength of 1,000–1,200 men, with Scottish regiments smaller at about 500 men. They were divided into companies of about 100 men, with those of the senior officers being larger (up to 200 men). In practice the numbers could be very variable. Each company would be distinguished by its flag, or colour, which formed a rallying point in the heat of battle (the origin of the continuing tradition of 'trooping the colour' to ensure that the men could recognise their own flag). The men of the New Model Army Foot were, for the first time, uniformly clothed in a single coat colour that has become famous as the British 'Redcoat'. Previously in the war regiments of both sides might be found wearing red, blue, green, grey or even white woollen coats. The militias, however, probably fought in their civilian clothes. The Scottish national army wore grey coats, although Charles II also had red-coated regiments at Worcester, including his Lifeguard. Officers would have worn their civilian clothes as a statement of their social rank.

At least two-thirds of an English Civil War infantry regiment at this time comprised musketeers, armed either with 12-bore matchlock muskets or, by 1651, with up to 20 per cent with flintlock muskets (firelocks). Both weapons had a range of 150 yards or so, with a trained musketeer capable of firing twice a minute. Although individual accuracy might be questionable during the heat of battle, such weapons could unleash devastating firepower when used rank upon rank and especially en masse, as in the contemporary tactic of firing a final salvee or volley. The musket was the real infantry killing machine on the Civil War battlefield. The Lowland Scots regiments were similarly armed but they would have faced severe problems of resupplying their men with powder and with the huge amount of saltpetre-soaked match needed to fire the matchlock muskets. A soldier could use 5cwt of match a day if on duty for long periods.[25] The vital necessity of maintaining a good supply of match for the Scots is especially important when considering the course of a battle which was to last over ten hours. This followed a march of three weeks in which they had been drawn into repeated skirmishing. By contrast, the Parliamentary army would have been able to replenish stocks easily. One shipment alone of match for the Parliamentary army at Worcester was for 30 tons. The remaining one-third of an infantry regiment was the pike division. The pikemen were considered socially superior to the musketeers and were used to protect the latter against cavalry attack or simply as a terror weapon, with the leaf-shaped points of the 16–18ft-long ash pikes aimed at the eyes of the enemy. Sir John Smythe, writing in 1595, left one of the best descriptions of the tactics used: 'with one puissant charge and thrust to enter and disorder, wound, open, and break the one with the other'.[26] This is a far cry from the harmless vertical wigwams of pike so beloved of some modern re-enactors! To protect the heads from simply being slashed off in combat they were protected by long strips of iron known as cheeks. At the start of the Civil Wars the pikemen wore a helmet and back- and breastplate. Tassets were attached to the breastplate in order to protect the thighs. By 1651 armour had commonly been discarded as it was heavy and offered little protection against musket shot.

The Highlanders were probably less well, or less consistently, equipped than the Lowland regiments, possibly armed only with dirk, sword or axe and a small shield. They also continued to use the more ancient technology of the longbow and were reviled for it by the English on their march south.[27] This was despite the fact that in trained hands the range of the longbow is greater than that of the musket and it has a faster rate of fire. Sir John Smythe remarked that 'archers are able to discharge four or five arrows apiece before the harquebusies shall be ready to discharge one bullet'.[28] The English had, however, lost the will to invest in the regular training from childhood that was required to develop a military archer. The stereotype of plaid-clad brigands should, however, be avoided and many of the Highlanders at Worcester were clearly armed with muskets. After Dunbar, Haselrigg said that he could only tell the Highlander and the Lowlander apart by the hardiness of the former, so they may have been dressed and equipped in similar fashion. Although the Highlanders certainly had a reputation for being less well-disciplined than the Lowland regiments that were organised into the national Scottish army, the romance of the wild Highland charge is probably a fallacy. It could merely have been a more exuberant form of the standard tactic of discharging weapons and then 'falling on' in the final assault.[29]

The Horse were the elite of seventeenth-century armies. The English were organised into 600-strong regiments, divided into troops of 100 men; the

Scottish cavalry regiments were smaller, with 450–500 men. By the time of the Civil War the cavalry were largely light horse, protected by back- and breastplate over a thick leather (buff) coat and a helmet. Both the English and Scots tried to resupply their Horse in 1651 with new armour: 1,000 sets of back- and breastplates and 1,500 helmets were ordered for the New Model Army in Scotland, and one Scottish regiment received 250 sets of armour sent from Sweden. The main use of the Horse was to break up enemy infantry formations (by attacking the flanks and rear), to take on the opposition Horse and then to harry any retreating forces. At Worcester, however, their use was to be hampered by the hedged landscape that prevented them from being deployed in large formations across the battlefield. Their primary weapon was a sword used for slashing. They would charge in close formation with drawn swords and, having broken the enemy's line, would then fire pistols or carbines at close range. Indeed, a pistol was commonly regarded as only being useful if fired at point-blank range. The Scots differed in also using lancers, as had been used in England in the sixteenth and earlier seventeenth centuries – and still a terrifying weapon in the minds of the opposing Foot.

The third type of soldier was a hybrid: the Dragoon. They rode into battle on lesser quality horses than the Horse but fought on foot, equipped as musketeers. They were especially useful for patrols, seizing key positions in advance of the main army and skirmishing as a rapid reaction force. None the less in November 1650 the regular Dragoon regiment of the New Model Army (Okey's) was converted into Horse. But it was soon realised that the army had lost flexibility by the change and other replacement regiments and troops of dragoons were quickly raised. On both sides a number of companies of Foot were converted to Dragoons during the course of the march south, presumably drawn from men who were already able to ride well. Cromwell would have converted more, but was concerned that this would alienate the local communities from whom the mounts would be requisitioned. It may be presumed that this was another cause for complaint against the Scots. Dragoons formed a mainstay of the militia regiments at Worcester and were to play a key role in the battle.

Severn Bridge) to provide musket-balls and the city was forced to supply iron to the value of £7 18s 1d to make cannon-balls, and another 2lb of steel for weapons.

By late August 1651 the King would have welcomed troops of any description. After the battle of Worcester Cromwell estimated the total number in the Royalist/Scottish army as around 16,000.[30] King Charles released Royalist gentry imprisoned within Worcester and made the traditional call to raise the *posse comitatus* of all able-bodied men aged between 16 and 60 in the county, to muster at Pitchcroft on 26 August. But the attendance was disappointing. Clarendon complained that even the 'well-affected' local gentry stayed away, along with others who had written letters of support prior to the campaign. Particular anger was directed against the 45-year-old Lord Coventry at Croome who, upon the approach of the King's army, conveniently retired to his sickbed. Charles II ordered him to be pulled 'out of his house by his ears' and sent troops to steal his horses! In similar vein the Presbyterian preacher Richard Baxter used the excuse of sore eyes not to come. This was already regarded by most people in England as a lost cause. In all, only 23 of the local gentry and 140 other men were listed as being present at the muster and some of these may have been inserted as a post-Restoration attempt to win favour from the new monarch. The final blow came when the handful of survivors of the Earl of Derby's defeat at Wigan slipped through the blockade and finally entered the city on 31 August. Derby brought just 250 Foot and 60 Horse. In all, probably no more than 2,000 Englishmen, described by the Council of State as 'the trash of the people', joined the Royalist cause at this time.[31] Those that did take part in the battle were die-hard Royalists, many of whom were Catholic and therefore reinforced the stereotype of the Cavaliers as circulated in Parliamentary propaganda. They formed a troop of Horse under Lord Talbot that, albeit small in numbers, was to play a crucial role in events. Nothing more symbolised that this had become a national conflict of England against Scotland than the fact that Charles chose to fight under the Scottish standard at the battle. But his was still not a united army and the proclamation of Charles II as Supreme Head of the Church by the former Dean, Dr Crosby, during a service at Worcester Cathedral on Sunday 24 September ignored the sensibilities of the Covenanters and only served to remind the English and Scots of their different ambitions.

Cromwell lost little time in containing the Scottish army, both to prevent any escape and to block any future recruitment or resupply. Despite the exhaustion of his men, a force under General Lambert was immediately sent the 15 miles to Upton-upon-Severn to secure the crossing over the

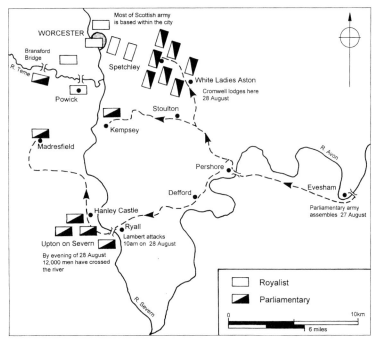

The line of march of the Parliamentary troops from Evesham to Upton-upon-Severn and Worcester on 27 August 1651.

Severn, block any further advance southwards and seize the exit routes west into Wales. The success of this mission would be crucial for the main battle to come. Meanwhile, the main army at Evesham held the crossing over the Avon and blocked any possibility of a break-out towards London.

Lambert's men marched through the night, eventually halting behind a low ridge just to the east of Upton, around the village of Ryall. Here they were out of sight of the Scots presumed to be guarding the Upton bridge. From this vantage point, on the morning of 28 August, Lambert was able to reconnoitre the wide river crossing and send out scouts. But through an inexplicable error the lax Scots (without the direct supervision of Massie) had not bothered to put a guard on the bridge, or the guard had slipped away to sleep. And so, in broad daylight at about 10am, Lambert ordered eighteen picked dragoons to establish a bridgehead, thus allowing the bridge to be repaired and the main force to cross over. The men first had to cross the open ground between Ryall and the riverside, then shuffle across the plank laid over the missing span of the bridge. The bridge at the time lay 82m south of the present bridge, south of the church. They successfully reached the other side but were then spotted and came under fire; they were forced to take cover in the adjacent church. The furious, and no doubt embarrassed, Scots attacked immediately, first firing their pistols through the church windows and then trying to set light to the building in order to burn the soldiers out. Unfortunately for them, all this served to do was to distract them from the fact that one of Lambert's scouting parties had found another crossing over the Severn, at a ford some 150m downstream, on Fisher's Row. From here, more dragoons forded the river and charged into the town. The Scots outside the church were outflanked and were forced to retreat along the main road towards Worcester. They probably made their last stand behind the earthwork constructed across the road on the outskirts of Upton but were outflanked by Horse and Dragoons charging along Hyde Lane to the west of their defences. Finds of musket-balls beside a hedgerow there probably indicate the point where the dragoons dismounted before their final assault. Massie was seriously wounded in trying to rally the rearguard before his men broke into a rout towards Worcester. He was reportedly shot in the left hand, right arm and thigh, and his horse was killed under him, by the fire of over forty carbines 'shot at him within half pistol shot'.

But there was no mad uncontrolled charge to follow them. Instead, Lambert ordered a halt and consolidated his position in Upton, making a temporary repair of the bridge and then sending back a message to Evesham for Fleetwood to bring reinforcements. Fleetwood sent over not only his own brigade but a reputed 12,000 men in total before nightfall, with musketeers from Corbett's regiment of Foot riding behind cavalry troopers in order to speed the process. Lambert sent out patrols under Colonel Blundell, Major Mercer and Captain Chappell to secure the immediate countryside. When Chappell's troops approached Madresfield House the small Scottish garrison there immediately retreated. It was then occupied by Captain Chappell's dragoons and twelve troopers of Horse, in order to protect the flanks of the main force when they eventually made their advance. Other troops, including New Model and Welsh Horse with Worcestershire Dragoons, under Colonels Twistleton and Kendrick, were also sent to seize the west side of the River Teme crossing at Bransford. This completed the encirclement by blocking the escape route into Wales, although the Scots evidently still held out some hopes of making an escape in this direction. They left the bridge intact until 1 September when they finally broke down the two outermost spans. The main force of Worcestershire Dragoons and Horse, along with two troops of Rich's

Flanking
attack

Upton-upon-
Severn church

Line of initial
assault

Aerial view of Upton-upon-Severn, looking north along the river. The site of the medieval bridge and the line of attack of the Parliamentary army on 28 September 1651 are indicated. (Photo: Mike Glyde)

Last stand
of Scots

Medieval bridge

Parliament
fords river

Aerial view of Upton-upon-Severn, looking north-east. The site of the medieval bridge and the line of attack of the Parliamentary army on 28 September 1651 are indicated. (Photo: Aerofilms)

Upton-upon-Severn church

Medieval bridge

Line of advance of Parliamentary army

The surviving church tower at Upton-upon-Severn. The Scots tried to burn out the initial Parliamentary assault force that took shelter here. This distracted them from the approach of the main Parliamentary army.

Horse, was also sent north to reinforce the Severn river crossing at Bewdley and prevent any retreat either into Wales or back north to Scotland. It may also be that Cromwell was putting some distance between the local troops and what was anticipated to be a bloody fight for their home city. This west part of the army was then allowed to rest in preparation for the final battle, while local barges and materials were commandeered ready to be dragged upstream to form two bridges of boats across the Severn and Teme at Worcester.

Lambert's dragoons charged up Oak Street and Fisher Lane (with what is now the Anchor Inn between them) from Fisher's Row towards the church at Upton-upon-Severn.

The remains of the shallow earthwork constructed by the Scots to block the road into Worcester from Upton-upon-Severn (the present B4211). This is where the Scots made their last stand.

Meanwhile, Cromwell had ordered the rest of the army with the main train of artillery to march towards Worcester while he and Fleetwood reconnoitred the countryside. This included riding down to Upton to congratulate Lambert and his men. Cromwell was greeted 'with abundance of joy and extraordinary shouting from his elated troops' before returning to his army on the east bank of the Severn.[32] This enormous army of up to 20,000 men now swept through the countryside along the roads and lanes, spilling out into the adjacent fields, past Pershore, Stoulton and White Ladies Aston in what had been described in 1644 as a 'woody and durty country'. Modern battle maps cannot fully represent the impact of such a large army on the march. Hedges would have been cleared to allow easy passage for the carts and artillery, and crops trampled. The army camped overnight in Spetchley Park on 29 August, just 2 miles south-east of Worcester, while Cromwell established a temporary headquarters at the house of the royalist Judge Berkeley.[33] His men are blamed for the defacing of some of the monuments in the church. The army then advanced to take up position on the crest of the hills surrounding Worcester, creating a front line some 4 miles in length. They met some resistance on the approach, as patrols of Scots tried to harry the advance as best they could from roadside ditches, hedgerows and trees. The Parliamentarian Colonel Stapleton reported how: 'Some small pickerings there was and poppings of musketeers behind the hedges but nothing considerable was attempted.'[34]

Now surrounded by an eager and confident Parliamentary army, the people of Worcester must have nervously considered their likely fate. On 1 September the Council of State warned that they were 'like to pay dear for their treason'.[35]

Chapter Three

Containment and Skirmishing Phase

The country came in freely to the Parliament's arm.[1]

28 August–2 September

With the river crossings on the Teme and Severn all in their control and the Scots surrounded, the bulk of the Parliamentary army could now rest and prepare for the final, inevitable, act of this drama. There was to be no parallel with the somewhat desultory 1646 siege of Worcester, when Parliament was content to contain the enemy for six weeks until they surrendered. At that time the gentlemanly nature of the siege even allowed the Parliamentary commander to invite his Royalist counterpart to dinner during a truce.[2] In 1651 the government could not risk Worcester becoming a focus for the Royalist cause in the country and were no doubt hoping for a rapid, decisive, victory.

On the west side of the city there must have been an atmosphere of a 'phoney war' because the troops were not in direct contact. This was a deliberate plan, possibly designed to lull the Scots into a false sense of security and to deceive them as to the total strength of the Parliamentary army on that side of the river. The Parliamentary outposts at Madresfield Court and Bransford Bridge would have been useful as a base from which to intercept any Scottish reconnaissance, supported by patrols from Upton-upon-Severn, and this tactic appears to have been successful. Certainly the evidence suggests that the Scots did not base any significant number of troops beside the river or fortify the riverbanks, despite the fact that there were thousands of the enemy camped just 9 miles away. Not only were the troops in St John's designed to act as a reserve in case there was an attack from that direction, but they could also be easily moved back into the city if the main attack came, as expected, from the east. Fleetwood and Lambert exchanged their commands as part of Cromwell's final troop dispositions. While Lambert returned to the army on the east side of Worcester, reuniting Cromwell with his second-in-command, Fleetwood once again took command of the men that he had sent to reinforce Lambert, now amounting to almost 50 per cent of the total strength of the army.

The Scots were evidently preparing to receive a major assault on the east side of the city, encouraged by the visible presence of large numbers of Parliamentary troops occupying the ring of high ground: the smoke from

53

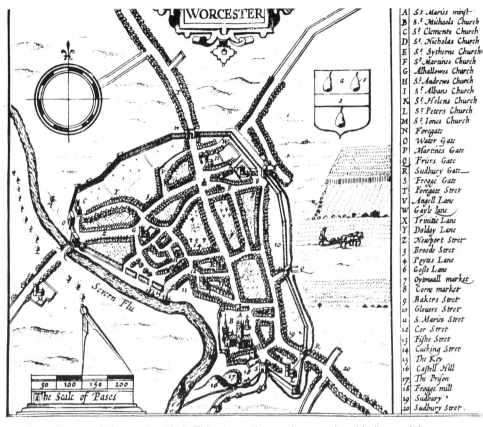

A	St Maries mint
B	St Michaels Church
C	St Clements Church
D	St Nicholas Church
E	St Sytherns Church
F	St Martines Church
G	Alhallowes Church
H	St Andrews Church
I	St Albans Church
K	St Helens Church
L	St Peters Church
M	St Iones Church
N	Foregate
O	Water Gate
P	Martines Gate
Q	Friers Gate
R	Sudbury Gate
S	Frogge Gate
T	Foregate Stret
V	Angell Lane
W	Gayle Lane
X	Trinitie Lane
Y	Dolday Lane
Z	Newport Stret
3	Broode Stret
4	Poytes Lane
6	Cosle Lane
7	Oytmeall market
8	Corne market
9	Bakers Stret
10	Glouers Stret
11	S. Maries Stret
12	Cor Stret
13	Fishe Stret
14	Cucking Stret
15	The Key
16	Castell Hill
17	The Prison
18	Frogge mill
19	Sudbury
20	Sudbury Stret

Speed's map of Worcester, 1610. This shows the castle mound and bailey and the extent of the pre-Civil War suburbs, which were largely destroyed during the conflict. Note also the site of the medieval bridge (north of the modern bridge) and the rows of houses leading to St John's on the east bank of the river. (By courtesy of Worcester City Museum)

their camp fires would have been seen rising through the trees. The Parliamentary army appeared to be settling in for a long siege. They built a defensive line that stretched from Elbury Hill in the north, on the high ground overlooking the River Severn and the main Scottish cavalry camp at Pitchcroft, through Perry Hill and Red Hill to Green Hill (with its vantage point of a windmill) and on to Bund's Hill in the south, overlooking the Severn. The recommended procedure in a siege was to build a series of camps defended by ramparts, ditches and stockades, on the model of Roman marching camps, linked by trench lines to contain the enemy. The nearest surviving examples of such siege lines are above Ludlow Castle, Shropshire. At Worcester the troops would have taken advantage of the natural topography, using the steep slopes and woodland as a natural defence, but adding a wooden palisade or trench along the crest of the hill. On Elbury Hill there was previously evidence for part of a rectangular enclosure 200 x 100 x 150 yards (182m x 91m x 137m); it was unfortunately destroyed in the nineteenth century but probably dates from this period. Blount also refers to a breastwork at the south end of Perry Wood, probably based on the line of a dried-up former watercourse.[3] There is still a surviving small rectangular emplacement (73m x 82m) on Tamar Place, off Newtown Road and Ronkswood Crescent, overlooking the city, which was probably an advanced troop emplacement. The feature known popularly as 'Cromwell's Trenches' on the north side of Perry Wood is, however, the remains of quarrying.[4] Tools for building siegeworks had been ordered up from Gloucester and the soldiers, with their notorious dislike of physical labour, impressed local civilians to dig the trenches. In 1646 only a proportion of the besieging troops had been held on the siege lines at any one time, with the rest (especially the Horse) quartered in farms and villages over a radius of 14 miles and this obviously eased the supply problem considerably. But in 1651, facing a larger enemy and with an assault or break-out expected imminently, it is likely that the army was held together on the siege lines. Unable to quarter themselves in the surrounding villages, the troops would have used the local woodland to make temporary shelters, as their predecessors in 1646 had done. Tents were not generally issued to troops on campaign in England, who were used to taking what shelter they could in woodland, hedgerows and ditches if it were not possible to billet themselves on local farms and villages. Three thousand tents had been supplied for the campaign in Scotland but these probably stayed with Monck. Some tents were ordered to be sent to Worcester (indicating that Parliament was anticipating a lengthy siege) but they failed to arrive before the battle and were immediately returned to London, leaving the army once again to fend for itself. The effort of maintaining an army of up to 18,000 men on the hills around Worcester cannot be under-estimated and it would have taken a major logistical operation to ensure that they were regularly supplied from the surrounding countryside. When Charles I camped a comparable army of 30,000 men in the Vale of Evesham in 1643, food had to be brought in from Shropshire.[5]

Map of the Civil War defences, as drawn in 1660. (By courtesy of Worcester City Library)

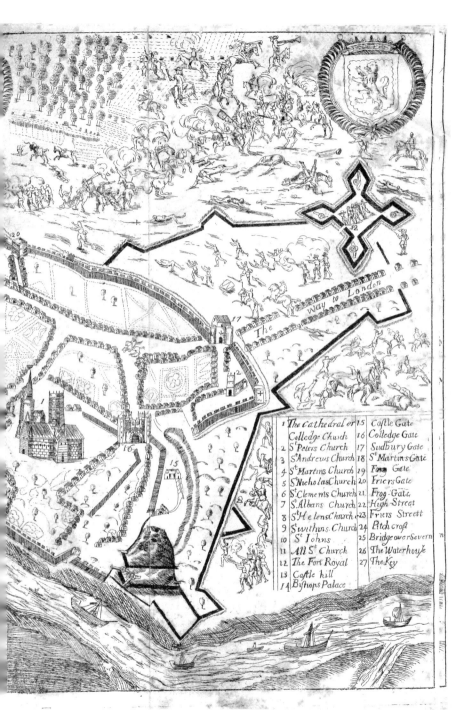

The Way to London

1	The Cathedral or Colledge Church	15	Castle Gate
2	St Peters Church	16	Colledge Gate
3	St Andrews Church	17	Sudbury Gate
4	St Martins Church	18	St Martins Gate
5	St Nicholas Church	19	Foregate
6	St Clements Church	20	Friers Gate
7	St Albans Church	21	Frog-Gate
8	St Helens Church	22	High Streett
9	St withins Church	23	Friers Streett
10	St Iohns	24	Pitch crosse
11	All St Church	25	Bridge over Severn
12	The Fort Royal	26	The Waterhouse
13	Castle hill	27	The Key
14	Byshops Palace		

Q Perspective View of the City,

Engraving of Worcester in 1764, looking over the River Severn from St John's. This clearly shows the ring of high ground to the east, which formed the basis of the

Cathedral of WORCESTER.

Parliamentary siege lines on that side of the city. (By courtesy of Worcester City Library)

The Scots deployed some of their troops under Middleton and Hamilton outside the east defences of the city, protected from attack by the network of drainage ditches in the marshy ground, so that in places the opposing forces were only 50 yards apart – 'half musket shot' – but this left them dangerously exposed. Cromwell therefore launched a series of artillery barrages against them and the city more generally, in order to test the defences and unsettle the defenders. Despite the fact that the Scots were largely reliant on the stocks of shot and powder that they had brought with them, they allowed themselves to be drawn into an artillery exchange that was no doubt deliberately designed to locate their cannon and deplete their stocks before the final assault. Naively the Scots returned fire from Fort Royal 'as if they never feared to want for powder or bullets'. The leather cannon that they had brought with them were not designed for prolonged barrages and it would not have been surprising if some of them had actually exploded! But there had been 28 cannon and 6 lighter drakes in the city during the siege of 1646, including a saker and a culverin, firing a $5^{1}/_{4}$ and 15lb cannon ball respectively. Some cannon of this size may have remained to be now reused by the Scots. Unfortunately, despite the leadership of their highly experienced General of Artillery James Wemyss (the former 'Master Gunner of England'), the gunners were described as being inexpert so it may be that they now had more guns than trained gunners. Cromwell's men also mounted a series of patrols to reconnoitre the enemy positions. One patrol sent to scout the area immediately outside the city walls on Sunday 31 August was led by Lambert and resulted in a fierce exchange of fire. All this activity would have inevitably led to the

Artillery emplacement on Tamar Place. This was either constructed during the siege of 1646 (and re-used in 1651) or newly built prior to the battle of Worcester in 1651.

conclusion, as intended, that this was to be the point at which Cromwell would mount his final assault.

The Scots did try to regain some of the initiative in the situation, perhaps guided in their tactics by the wounded Massie, who had followed the same methods in his successful defence of Gloucester in 1643. Then his heavily outnumbered men had broken the spirit of the besieging Royalists. In that instance, the odds seemed at first sight even more hopeless, with Massie having only 1,500 men against a Royalist force of 30,000. But night after night his men had launched sallies against the besiegers, sometimes involving around one-third of the garrison. They had stormed trenches and destroyed artillery positions, and even made amphibious assaults, fighting almost to their last barrel of gunpowder. Many of the Royalists in Worcester in 1651 must have clung desperately to the success of this precedent and indeed King Charles's later efforts to mount a pincer attack against the besiegers is very reminiscent of Massie's tactics at Gloucester.[6] But this was not the divided country of 1643 and Cromwell's army was very different from the sick and hungry Royalists that had surrounded Gloucester. The Scots launched a series of raids against the surrounding Parliamentary troops but, illustrating just how far events were in Cromwell's control, their plans were immediately betrayed by informers within the city. Thus, on 29 August General Middleton and Sir William Keith mounted a major night raid of over 1,000 Foot and 250 Horse on the main Parliamentary position on Red Hill and the southern outpost on Bund's Hill. They wore their white shirts over their coats and armour as an identification signal in what was known as a camisado (although usually this consisted merely of pulling out the shirt tail, so that the white was only visible to troops of one's own side, coming up behind). Unfortunately for the raiding party a local tailor, William Guise, was also a Parliamentary spy and had climbed over the walls of Worcester using a knotted rope to warn the Parliamentary troops about the raid before returning to the city. The Parliamentary troops had consequently withdrawn their outposts and were waiting in an ambush for the Royalist Scots. The white shirts made a good target from all directions. Musketeers hidden behind the hedgerows opened fire and ten men were killed on Bund's Hill, their bodies found the next day on the Kempsey Road (now the A38). A further half-dozen soldiers here were taken prisoner. On Red Hill the Royalists faced Sir Charles Fairfax's regiment of Foot and tried desperately to escape the trap set for them. As the ambush was sprung, Major Knox tried to break out of the lane and 'coming very boldly up, and leaping over a hedge, rushed upon a stand of pikes, and so [as his victors termed it] lost his life in a vapour'.[7] The Parliamentary victory was not without its cost: unfortunately for William Guise, he was captured upon his return and executed – hanged from the signboard of the Golden Cross Inn on Broad Street. Despite this warning, other Parliamentary spies continued to operate in the city, controlled by the Parliamentary Scout-Master. They included one woman, enigmatically referred to as a 'little maid', and were subsequently rewarded with payments of up to £100. As a consequence, Cromwell had excellent intelligence as to the disposition of the Scottish army. Other patrols of Scottish Horse that were attempting to reconnoitre on the west side of the city were similarly intercepted and were turned back near Bransford Bridge by Parliamentary forces on the night of Monday 1 September. One of the casualties in this phase of skirmishing may have been a soldier who was described as being shot in the head a few days before the main battle. The army surgeon Richard Wiseman conducted brain surgery on him, trepanning the skull to extract the musket-ball and removing part of the damaged brain. Remarkably, the patient, who was conscious throughout the procedure, survived the immediate operation, living at least to 3 September.[8]

News of the failure of the sallies spread quickly, convincing any possible doubters as to the strength and ability of the Parliamentary forces. Now 'the country came in freely to the Parliament's army' in order to be seen to have supported what was expected to be the winning side.[9] This irregular force was the successor of the *posse comitatus* – the expectation of all males aged 16 to 60 to bear arms in times of crisis. Significantly, King Charles had made a futile attempt to raise the same men when he had first arrived in Worcester. Indeed, all previous attempts by the Royalists in Worcestershire to raise the *posse comitatus* during the Civil Wars had met with an almost equally poor response. But now there was a chance to end the threat of war

Red Hill and Perry Wood from Worcester Cathedral tower (with Fort Royal to the right).

once and for all and to take revenge on what was seen as the unholy alliance of war-mongering Scots and fanatical Royalists. In sharp contrast to the increasing Parliamentary confidence, inside the city morale declined even further, compounded by the realisation that the Earl of Derby's defeat at Wigan had removed any possibility of relief or further rising. Clarendon described the encircled army as being in a state of 'amazement and confusion'. The Royalists were trapped in a city at best ambivalent to their cause, hundreds of miles from home and facing a doubtful fate if Parliament made an attack. Under the rules of contemporary warfare, if a castle or town under siege refused the offer of surrender and an outright assault was made then the lives of all within, civilian and soldier alike, would be considered forfeit and the place itself open to wholesale pillage. In these circumstances even Massie's servant deserted him and fled to the Parliamentary army for sanctuary. The tensions already present within the Scottish forces deepened: Scottish infantry especially were described as being mutinous, prophetically fearing that the Horse would run and leave them to their fate.[10] The citizens of Worcester must have felt entirely helpless with their only hope being the early surrender of the Scots and the chance to throw themselves on Cromwell's mercy. In 1646 the Royalist garrison had finally been obliged to surrender, fearing, with good reason, that the citizens were about to rise up against them. In 1651 the Scottish army was too large for this to be considered – but none the less one can imagine the Scottish soldiers facing dark looks in the streets and within their billets, and hints that perhaps they should take their fight elsewhere! In clear echoes of the city's feelings in both 1642 and 1646, Colonel Stapleton reported that the citizens 'curse the cavaleers, and repent that they ever deserted the Parliament'.[11]

Rations within the city were probably already running low, with any available food being requisitioned by the army. The citizens later claimed that they had been 'enforced and compelled' to provide food and supplies for the Scots, at a cost of £183 14s 4d, including veal, mutton, lamb, chicken, rabbit, pigeon, duck, eggs, butter, hams, bread, fruit, candles and wine. On the night before the battle the city spent £7 5s 4d on wine for the troops. On the day of the battle itself they spent £6 4s 8d on food and a further £6 6s on 9 gallons of sack and over 11 gallons of claret to fortify the troops. This must have severely strained resources and further distanced the citizens from their unwelcome guests. Outside the city the besiegers were receiving a more enthusiastic reception, albeit tinged with relief that the battle was being fought on someone else's doorstep! On 1 September Gloucester sent 16,000 loaves of bread and 40 barrels of 'stronge beere' to the Parliamentary army and a barrel of better quality 'double beer' for Cromwell.

Meanwhile, in the Parliamentary camp crucial preparations for the impending battle could be made well away from the gaze of the Scots. On 31 August Cromwell held a council of war with his generals to finalise the battle plan. The outline was then passed to the Council of State and even to militia committees across the country so that all in the Parliamentary organisation were prepared for the coming events.[12] The known events suggest that the intended plan involved a slow, careful, build-up over a number of distinct stages. One crucial key to success would be effective communications over what would be an 8-mile front. There is evidence to suggest that the action on 3 September was only intended as the first stage of a more protracted campaign aimed at total and absolute victory. Hence Parliament sent up a consignment of tents in readiness for a long siege and blockade. But Cromwell was to demonstrate flexibility in his generalship. In the event, he was able to seize the opportunity of the moment and bring all to a conclusion within a single day. One advantage to the Parliamentary planning was that Charles had only hazy ideas as to where the main Parliamentary forces were concentrating, and therefore from which direction the main thrust of the battle would be coming. This was not to be a classic English Civil War battle laid out on an open battlefield with the opposing armies directly facing each other. Forming an arc around the east side of the city, some 18,000 troops were hidden behind the screen of woodland on the line of hills. Just 9 miles away at Upton another huge army of 12,000 men was gathering and twenty barges were commandeered; these would provide the framework for two pontoon bridges, ready to be dragged up-river and thrown across the Teme and Severn. These bridges would provide the essential means of battlefield communication for an engagement that would be fought across an 8-mile front bisected by two major rivers. Planks and other timberwork also needed to be collected, cut and pre-fabricated, and mooring ropes made.

Engineers of the time were highly skilled in building such bridges. A contemporary description of 'bridges of boats' was provided by Robert Ward in 1639. He described similar bridges made in the Netherlands which were 20–23ft (6–7m) long and broad enough for four men to march abreast. These were major feats of battlefield engineering. The pontoons had to be dragged into position, anchored in the water, weighed down and securely tied to the opposing banks. Ramps had to be constructed to provide easy access up the steep riverbanks. The piles for the mooring points, driven deep into the bed of the river, must have been substantial as they are reputed to have survived until the end of the nineteenth century.[13] The construction and use of such bridges was well known in the region. The Royalists had built several across the Severn at Tewkesbury in 1643 (Prince Maurice), while the

A contemporary illustration of the pontoons used as the basis of the type of 'bridge of boats' used at Worcester. From Robert Ward's Animadversions of Warre *(1639). (By courtesy of Brown University Library)*

Parliamentary side had constructed them at Framilode (William Waller), and at the siege of Worcester in 1646 (Edward Whalley). It is difficult now to reconstruct the nature of the seventeenth-century River Severn. The construction of weirs and locks, modern dredging and the accumulation of some 350 years of rapid alluvial build-up from annual flooding have radically changed the river profile. In the seventeenth century it was shallower, with a number of fords across it. The bridge builder of 1646, Edward Whalley, was now commanding a regiment of Horse in Cromwell's army. His practical experience and local knowledge of the river conditions would have been invaluable to Cromwell. It is even possible that the piles for his own bridge of 1646, built to the north of the Severn Bridge, still survived and were intended to be rebuilt later in the campaign. But what distinguishes the bridges made at Worcester in 1651 was the effort required to drag them all the way from Upton and then the speed with which they were to be completed, under fire, in the heat of battle.

The Parliamentary artillery barrage from the east side of Worcester escalated on 2 September, pounding the Royalist positions on that side of the city. Charles and his generals reached the obvious (and intended) conclusion that an assault from that direction was imminent. They remained in their saddles most of the night, listening for the signs of the attack at dawn – but they were deceived.[14]

Chapter Four

The Opening Attack

This is the day of the Lord God of Hosts, a day of vengeance, his sword shall devour his enemies, it will be drenched with their blood.[1]

Noon, 3 September

Wednesday 3 September, the first anniversary of Cromwell's victory against the Scottish army at Dunbar, opened as a clear and fine day, although some accounts tell of a thundery atmosphere. The significance of the date would not have been lost on anyone either in Worcester or beyond. Back in the homes of the commanders of the Essex militia, the family of Colonel Cooke at Pebmarsh had spent the previous day in prayer and on the Wednesday the Honeywood family were also praying for Sir Thomas and his men in anticipation of the coming battle.[2] There was a clear air of expectation across the country. But after the fierce barrage of the previous day the morning was strangely quiet and King Charles had received reports that enemy troops under Colonel Barton had been drawn off towards Bewdley and others sent to Upton-upon-Severn. The actuality was that the troops at Bewdley were being stationed to block any Scottish retreat following the battle, while those sent to Upton had joined Fleetwood's assault force. Cromwell was clearly satisfied with the strength of his forces on the east side of Worcester to make these final troop dispositions away from the city. But as well as lulling the King into thinking that there would not be an imminent attack, the news may even have been leaked to the Royalists in order to tempt them out of the city. Charles held a council of war with his generals to discuss the latest situation. The meeting was held on top of the Cathedral tower, where they had a panoramic view of the city. It would have been a crowded meeting. One of the problems of the Royalist side was that they had a multiplicity of generals, all fighting to express their opinion and wracked with rivalry. They included Leslie and Middleton (Covenanter and Engager, who detested each other), Hamilton, Montgomery and Pitscottie, the English Buckingham and Massie, James Wemyss (the General of Artillery), and even a Dutch mercenary and former engineer officer, Jonas Van Drusche, who commanded a cavalry brigade. In addition there were the nobility, including the Earl of Derby and six other earls. There were Covenanters, Engagers, former Parliamentarians as well as confirmed Royalists. By

Worcester Cathedral from Fort Royal. King Charles used the 52m-high tower as his command post during much of the battle.

contrast, Cromwell's army maintained a much tighter command structure under Fleetwood, Deane, Lambert and Harrison; the leaders shared a common past and experience, with three being regicides (those who had signed Charles I's death warrant).

The possibility of the Royalists mounting their own attack against what was thought to be a weakened enemy on the east side of the city was discussed at the meeting. As Cromwell and the Council of State had predicted before the battle (see below), there were only two main options for the beleaguered Scots. With supplies dwindling, they could either risk waiting out a siege in the hope that further support from the nation would come to them, or try to break out and capture the capital – London. Even putting aside Cromwell's superiority in numbers, the immediate landscape around Worcester was not suitable for contemplating a set-piece, large-scale and open battle. The land to the west was enclosed by hedges and to the east the boggy, ditched enclosures led on to wooded hills: both made large-scale deployment in the classic form of Edgehill, Marston Moor or Naseby difficult, especially for Horse. It is unlikely that Charles would have received any decisive or consistent advice from his depressed and divided generals, who were no doubt themselves thinking back to the events of one year before. Leslie, at least, was probably already pondering as to the best way of engineering an escape for his men back to

CHRONOLOGY OF THE BATTLE OF WORCESTER

NB: All timings are approximate

5am	Parliamentary army under Fleetwood leaves Upton
12 noon	West column attacks Powick Bridge
2pm	East column reaches confluence of Teme and Severn
3pm	Cromwell attacks across bridge of boats
4pm	King Charles counter-attacks on east side of city but is repulsed
5pm	Fort Royal captured and Sidbury Gate stormed
6pm	Charles II escapes from the city
8pm	Most of Scots surrender
10pm	Last of Royalist army surrenders

Scotland. As a consequence Charles took personal command during the battle – the fate of 16,000 men and the future of his kingdom were weighty responsibilities for his young shoulders. Lulled into thinking that there would be no attack on them so late in the morning, the Royalist officers avoided making a decision by dispersing to the inns of the city for their luncheons! This was strangely reminiscent of the events prior to the battle of Dunbar, when the officers had left their men in the field at a critical time. They were, however, unaware that the military machine of the Parliamentary army had been on the move since dawn and was gearing up for the attack.

Cromwell's choice of 3 September for the start of the battle can hardly have been a coincidence, and he was to reinforce the symbolism. The Parliamentary watchword for the battle was to be 'The Lord of Hosts', as used in the preceding year in their triumph at Dunbar. The biblical message behind the slogan was clear for the Scots to understand: 'This is the day of the Lord God of Hosts, a day of vengeance, his sword shall devour his enemies, it will be drenched with their blood' (Jeremiah 46:10). All were aware that they were going to be taking part in the final deciding battle of the Civil Wars and the Parliamentary side fervently believed that they were instruments of divine will. The field sign was to be that no one should show anything white, probably because at the recent battle at Wigan the Royalists had used white ribbons as their recognition sign (and 'Jesus' as their watchword). By now what were rather grubby white shirt collars were presumably tucked into the soldiers' coats. The main purpose of this was presumably to avoid any confusion between the non-uniformed Parliamentary militias and the English Royalists. However, this instruction reached less than one-third of the Parliamentary troops and proved to be unnecessary as the majority of the enemy were the Scots in their hodden grey coats or Highland plaid and ubiquitous blue bonnets.[3] But the Scottish Lifeguard and at least one other regiment were clothed in red. The King had tried to re-equip his ragged army at Worcester as best he could in the days before the battle. The local draper, Henry Wright, provided £453 1s 5d of red and grey cloth to the army on 2 and 3 September, although there would have been no time to have it made up into uniforms. He had only been paid with a promissory note and so had particular cause

CHARLES FLEETWOOD (1618–92)

Charles Fleetwood was commander of the Parliamentary Horse during the 1651 campaign and led the attack on the west side of Worcester. He was born in Northamptonshire in 1618. A late-comer to the Parliamentary cause, he became a member of the Earl of Essex's Lifeguard and fought at Newbury in 1643. He commanded a cavalry regiment at Naseby in 1645. Fleetwood was a radical within the New Model Army and was also elected as an MP in 1646. He is reputed to have been the principal author of the plot to seize King Charles I at Holmby, but he did not take part in the trial against the King, which meant that he escaped the fate of the regicides. Fleetwood became a member of the Council of State in 1651 and was responsible for raising the militia forces in England to support Cromwell's campaign. After the battle of Worcester Fleetwood became Commander in Chief in Ireland until he was recalled in 1655 following complaints that he was favouring Anabaptists and other extreme puritan sects. He then became one of Cromwell's major-generals, responsible for the eastern counties. Married to one of Cromwell's daughters (Bridget, widow of Henry Ireton) in 1652, Fleetwood was considered to be Oliver's likely natural successor, although at first he supported Richard Cromwell. In 1659 Fleetwood joined Desborough and Lambert to help remove Richard Cromwell as Lord Protector, following Richard's failure to accede to the demands of the army. Fleetwood was appointed Commander in Chief of the army but was then replaced by General Monck. He outlived the Restoration and died in 1692 as the last surviving Parliamentary general.

to despair of the events of 3 September. His widow was still trying to claim payment in 1675.

The immediate objective of the stage of the battle that was planned for 3 September is arguable and it is likely never to have been Cromwell's intention to capture the city in a single day. Instead the goal was probably to simply secure the west side of Worcester and enable a tight siege of the city. Unknown to the Scots, the Parliamentary force from Upton-upon-Severn, now under the command of General Fleetwood and well rested since their occupation of the town on 28 August, had begun to move up the 9 miles towards Worcester before dawn. Their line of march was screened from any enemy patrols by the advance guard established at Madresfield and there are no reports of any contact with the Scots until the army was almost at the Teme. At this stage the Teme crossing was protected only by a small brigade of Highlanders under Sir William Keith at Powick Bridge and another force of just 300 Highlanders under Major-General Colin Pitscottie at the junction of the Teme and Severn. There may have been three further brigades of Foot and Horse, amounting to 2,000–2,500 men in reserve in St John's, under Montgomery and Dalziel. The Parliamentary army advanced north in two columns. The smaller west column under Major-General Richard Deane (Cobbett's and Haynes' Foot with Matthew's Foot in reserve and with Fleetwood's Horse) headed for the ridge of high ground and the vantage point of the tower of Powick church. From there they hoped to be in a position where they could quickly sweep down into the floodplain and across the narrow stone Powick Bridge over the Teme. But it had been recognised that the advance could not rely on a single crossing-point. Therefore the east column under Fleetwood advanced along the banks of the Severn, dragging the twenty barges and planking against the river current, ready to make pontoon bridges across the Teme and the Severn. The pontoon bridge across the Teme would support the attack across Powick Bridge, and the bridge across the Severn would link the armies on both sides of the river and offer a means of attacking the Scots' flank. Both bridges could be protected by a common bridgehead in the angle of the two rivers, using the adjacent hedgerows as cover. Once they had crossed the River Teme then both columns could sweep into St John's and occupy the west bank of the Severn opposite the city. This may have been the extent of the ambition for what was planned as only the first stage of the battle, leaving the city tightly surrounded on all sides and with little chance for the Scottish army to escape. Consequently, there is no evidence that Cromwell issued a formal order for the city to surrender on 3 September, which would have been the normal prelude to a major assault, and this was to spare the lives of the citizens.

Cromwell, advised by local officers and experienced campaigners such as Colonel Whalley, would already have seen the enclosed, hedged landscape around the Teme from his vantage point on Bund's Hill to the east. As the subsequent accounts from his officers testify, this network of small fields, river meadows, orchards and hopyards was clearly not a suitable terrain to tempt the Scots into open battle. The patchwork of hedged and ditched fields would render the use of Horse very difficult and indeed the majority of the New Model Army Horse were drawn up on the east side of the city. It is true that English soldiers did have a high reputation among the Scots for their skill in fighting in such conditions. In 1648 the Scots had deliberately chosen to invade through Yorkshire rather than Lancashire because the enclosed county of Lancashire would give an advantage to the New Model Army's 'experienced and well trained sojors and excellent firemen'.[4] But this was a type of landscape that gave the advantage to defenders. The well-advertised presence of the army on the east side of the city would, it was hoped, ensure that the King did not draw off all his troops to engage Fleetwood's troops. If by any chance the Scots did take significant numbers of soldiers from the city, then this would give Cromwell the option of mounting an attack from his positions on the east of the city, although a frontal assault on substantial defences was always going to be risky and costly in lives. But Charles was not tempted to throw substantial reinforcements into the battle on the west side of the city and in the event Cromwell made no attempt to launch an assault against the east defences until his hand was forced in the late afternoon (around 5pm). To commence a major phase of a battle so late in the day was not unknown at the time, but it would be unlikely. The battle of Dunbar (September 1650) began before dawn at around 4am, Naseby (June 1645) between 10am and 11am, Cropredy Bridge (June 1644) around 1pm, Edgehill (October 1642) between 2pm and 3pm. But at Marston Moor (July 1644) the battle may have begun as late as 7pm, lasting until about 9pm. It would, however, still have been light at that time of the year, whereas at Worcester in September the final attack on the city took place at dusk, with fighting extending well into the hours of darkness, suggesting an act of opportunism rather than a predetermined plan.

Cromwell's plan for 3 September was probably limited to driving the Scots out of St John's and then occupying the west bank of the Severn, moving one of the pontoon bridges up the river to provide closer support. He may even have considered building an additional bridge north of the Severn Bridge, as had happened in the siege of 1646, to try to link the armies across the north side of the city. This would threaten the Scottish Horse from opposite directions and provide the means for a subsequent stage of battle, with three potential crossings on the west side of the city which could be combined with simultaneous attacks on the gates on the east side, all supported by heavy siege cannon. But the storming of a town across ditches and over stone walls and earthen ramparts was likely to be a bloody affair. Once contained, the fate of the city could have been left to a blockade – as had happened most recently at the siege of Colchester in 1648 – although the prospect of a long siege at Worcester was thought unlikely. The thinking of Cromwell and the Council of State is clearly shown in correspondence before the battle. The Council of State had written to General Blake, commander of the navy, appraising him of the situation, explaining that the bridge of boats would be used to link up Cromwell's and Fleetwood's armies and then 'we shall speedily force them to fight, or starve, or run if they can break through; the latter will be most likely'. In similar vein on 2 September the Council of State wrote to the Militia Commission of Yorkshire that a 'few days will put them to a necessity either to fight or fly, and the latter is most likely'.[5] It was clearly thought that a desperate attempt would be made to break out of the city before they starved. Once the west bank was secured (giving the Scots only one exit point in their control), then this could only be to the north or east, where reserves and the bulk of the Horse were waiting to intercept them.

Although the Parliamentary order of battle is not complete and is at times contradictory in the contemporary accounts, it seems clear that Fleetwood's formations were based on militia regiments brigaded together with hardened New Model Army troops. This was a sensible arrangement in view of the long-standing suspicion of the value of the militia. Indeed, it can be argued that Cromwell intended the militia to be used as the initial shock troops – cannon fodder to protect the New Model Army regiments in the final assault. The force was mainly Foot, with some support from Horse and Dragoons. Fleetwood had up to 12,000 men in total under his command. The scale of artillery support is not known, although the finds of cannon balls in Powick and beside Manor Farm show that light field guns at least were present. If so, it is likely that they would have mainly fired anti-personnel case-shot, which may be mis-identified as musket-balls (although it tends to be more angular).

On the east side of the river another 15,000 men under Lambert and Harrison were drawn up on the ridge overlooking the city, from Elbury Hill south through Battenhall to Bund's Hill, near what is now the Ketch Inn. This included the main force of Parliamentary cavalry, clearly placed to oppose the main Scottish Horse concentration on Pitchcroft. Cromwell also retained a reserve of 3,000 crack New Model Army Horse and Foot under his command, positioned on the left flank behind Bund's Hill to

JOHN LAMBERT (1619–83)

John Lambert was born in Yorkshire in 1619 and trained to become a lawyer. He joined the Parliamentary side at the start of the Civil War and directed the siege of Skipton Castle. By 1643 he was a colonel in the besieged town of Hull. An army radical, in 1647 he was a spokesman for the army in seeking arrears of pay and indemnity for past actions before committing them to go to Ireland. In June he was one of the commissioners preparing the ultimately unsuccessful Heads of Proposals to settle the peace. He fought alongside Cromwell at the battle of Preston in 1648. He was not, however, involved in the trial or execution of Charles I. In June 1650 Lambert, now a major-general, was appointed second-in-command of the army, fighting at Dunbar, Edinburgh, Leith and Burntisland. His capture of the river crossing at Upton-upon-Severn was crucial for the success of the battle of Worcester. On 9 September the House of Parliament resolved: 'That lands of inheritance in Scotland, to the yearly value of one thousand pounds sterling, be settled upon Major-General Lambert and his heirs, for his great and eminent services for its commonwealth.' Lambert was then sent to Edinburgh to endeavour to make a final settlement between England and Scotland. In 1653 he was elected as an MP and in December 1653 was chosen to formally offer the title of Lord Protector to Cromwell. He later proposed that this title be made hereditary (although opposing the suggestion that Cromwell should be given the kingship). But Lambert then fell out of favour with Cromwell and retired to private life. Following Cromwell's death Lambert was re-elected as an MP. After the resignation of Richard Cromwell as Lord Protector he commanded the suppression of the Royalist risings. Lambert opposed Monck's march into England and was captured at Daventry by Ingoldsby. This ardent republican remained in prison after the Restoration until his death in 1683.

guard that flank and ready to be used on whichever side of the river they seemed most urgently needed. They comprised the Lifeguard, Cromwell's and Hacker's Horse, and Ingoldsby's and Charles Fairfax's Foot (who had been stationed on Bund's Hill since 28 August), supported by Goffe's and Deane's Foot. Charles Fairfax was the elderly uncle of the former Commander-in-Chief, Thomas Fairfax. Cromwell's headquarters during the morning may have been in a cottage on the edge of Perry Wood. According to later legend, this is where he sold his soul to the devil in return for victory and seven more years of power.[6]

River Teme

Powick bridge

Aerial view of Powick, looking north. (Photo: Aerofilms)

Scottish retreat

Powick church

Line of advance of
Parliamentary army

RICHARD DEANE (1610–53)

Deane came from a Gloucestershire puritan family. He served as General of Artillery to the Earl of Essex's army and then as Comptroller of Ordnance to the New Model Army. As such, he was in command of the artillery at Naseby. He served in Cromwell's campaign in Wales and at the battle of Preston during the Second Civil War. Deane was a regicide and in 1649 was appointed a Commissioner of the Navy. He commanded the fleet that supported Cromwell's army in the Dunbar campaign. After the battle of Worcester he was appointed as President of the Commission for the Settlement of Scotland. He returned to sea during the Anglo-Dutch war and was killed while serving as 'General-at-sea' in the battle of North Foreland in 1653.

The tower of Powick church showing (inset) the impact marks of musket-balls on the north face.

The first notice of the approach of Fleetwood's army may have been at the ford across Carey's Brook on the Upton Road below Powick. Here local tradition tells of Fleetwood's cavalry pausing to water their horses, and a number of burials may indicate the site of a skirmish. The burials were, however, undated and Romano-British burials are also known from the area. The pikemen may have tried to make their 16–18ft-long pikes less conspicuous by carrying them at a shallow angle on their shoulders or 'trailing' them behind them from waist height, with their armour dulled by painting or russeting (controlled rusting which gives a brown colour to armour) to prevent it glinting in the sunlight; but the scale of the approaching army marching across the undulating landscape would soon have become clear to the men in the observation post established on the roof of Powick church tower. Troops were sent to dislodge the Scots from church and churchyard, as testified by the marks of musket-balls or case-shot on the wall of the tower. Whether the shocked Scots regained their lines to provide a warning is not known, but Deane's column then found itself foiled by the natural defensive position of the landscape from Powick leading down to the river, a distance of just over half a mile (1km). Arriving around midday, the cavalry of Fleetwood's regiment found it difficult to deploy in the narrow hedged lanes in the area, particularly around Powick itself and the land to the west. The hedged landscape of Powick and the approach to St John's was to be a major frustration for the Parliamentary forces, repeatedly commented upon in contemporary accounts. The Doharty Map of 1741, eighteenth-century estate maps and the tithe map of 1840 all show a landscape of complex fields and closes that had probably not greatly changed from the seventeenth to the late nineteenth century. They probably dated from early enclosure in the medieval period. The floodplain immediately adjacent to the Rivers Severn and Teme had larger paddocks and open fields that would make the forming-up of troops easier, but the fields on the north side of the Teme (in what is now an extension of St John's) were again small and were to cause further problems for the Parliamentary troops during the day. The anticipated rapid advance slowed and the small number of Scottish troops who had been based on the south side of the Teme retreated only with a determined resistance 'at push of pike' down the enclosed lanes. Close combat in such circumstances was the best way of negating the firepower of their enemy. The fighting was described as 'very hot, but the Lord gave our men to gaine ground of the enemy, till we had beaten them out of the ground'.[7] Nineteenth-century field names in Powick parish record 'Killing Acre', 'Slaughter Furlong' and 'King's End', which may hark back to the events of the battle and give an idea of the half-mile front over which Deane's

Powick Ham, looking towards Powick church, which is sited on the end of a low ridge of high ground. The church was used as a forward observation post by the Scots.

brigade advanced. Just below the church finds of musket-balls and a small cannon ball behind what is now the Red Lion public house, and 'Slaughter Furlong' to the east, illustrate the rolling engagement as Deane's men fought yard by yard the 918 yards (840m) to the river.

When Deane's brigade finally reached the Teme they found that Keith's Highlanders had demolished the two furthest spans of the bridge. The Scots were able to cover the crossing from the nearby mill buildings (now rebuilt as the converted power station) and from Hobmore Hill (possibly defended with entrenchments) behind it. The steep slopes of the Teme made it difficult to make a crossing elsewhere; to get troops across the river they would therefore be largely reliant on the completion of the two bridges of boats that were being dragged up the river. But the east column under Fleetwood, comprising the New Model Army regiments of Gibbon and Blake, together with the militia regiments of Marsh and Grey, had also faced difficulty in reaching their objective. They had to drag the heavy pontoons against the strong current of the Severn, and the pioneers

The approach lane to Powick Bridge. This gives a good impression of the narrow hedged lanes that proved so difficult for the cavalry. The Scots fought a hand-to-hand retreat down such lanes to Powick Bridge.

repeatedly had to cut a passage through the hedges that ran down to the riverbank. They finally reached the confluence with the Teme at around 2pm. This is just under a mile (1.5km) east of Powick Bridge. Here they faced only some 300 men under Pitscottie, but these proved enough to prevent a rapid crossing. As the advance of both columns came to a halt on the bank of the Teme, with the Parliamentary army forming up in clear view on the floodplain, the air would have been filled with the angry buzz of musket-balls corkscrewing through the air and the pungent smell of black powder. But now the superior firepower of the Parliamentary army seemed of little use and they simply could not get men across the natural defence of the river. The broad loop of the River Teme created a natural bastion and allowed the small numbers of Scottish musketeers to fire into the flanks of the advancing Parliamentary army. The initial element of surprise and rapid advance had been lost, and Charles had been given the opportunity to reinforce his men.

A near-contemporary illustration of seventeenth-century troops advancing at point of pike, with 16ft-long pikes levelled at the eyes of the enemy (a far cry from the harmless 'wigwams' carried aloft by many modern re-enactors!). Behind them are the cavalry. Detail from Speed's map of Worcester, 1610. (By courtesy of Worcester City Museum)

The first news of the attack brought panic to the Royalist army within the city. At first they thought that this was only a small diversionary force of about 1,000 men, with the main Parliamentary attack still expected to come from the east. Caught unawares, the King only began to send reinforcements to Keith and Pitscottie as the Parliamentary troops were advancing down the ridge from Powick. In the race to reach the Teme, it was only the previous part-demolition of Powick Bridge that saved the Scots from an early disaster. Just a few of Keith's musketeers could defend the narrow crossing-point from the shelter of the adjacent mill and high ground behind. Although an attack had obviously been expected at some point, now the moment of truth had actually arrived the Royalists were sent into an immediate panic. King Charles, in the city centre, was almost knocked down by some of his cavalry 'running in so great disorder, that he could not stop them, though he used all the means he could, and called to many officers by their names'.[8] Once again Charles rushed up to the top of the 52m-high tower of the Cathedral, with its 235 steps. But from that distance, even with 'prospective glasses', all he would have seen was the

80

Powick Bridge from the east. Keith's command post was in the mill on the site of the present converted power station.

clouds of gunpowder smoke beginning to rise from the fields to the south, obscuring his view of events. After calling up immediate reinforcements from Major-General Robert Montgomery's troops in St John's, he therefore rode down to the Teme to see for himself and exhort his men. Although his later reputation is as a flamboyant figure, that day he was dressed simply and soldierly in a buff coat over a linen doublet, with back- and breastplate and grey breeches. Only the Order of the Garter around his neck distinguished him as the monarch. Throughout the day he was to ride back and forth across the battlefield trying to inspire his men. Although reports of his personal bravery were no doubt emphasised for their propaganda value, there does seem no doubt that he was making a determined effort to

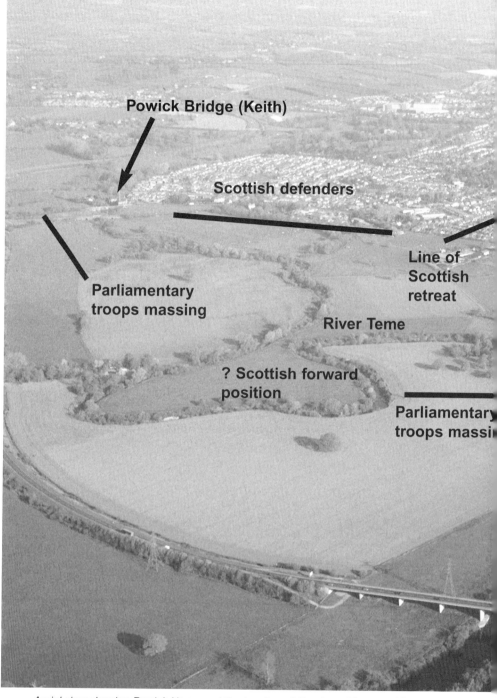

Powick Bridge (Keith)

Scottish defenders

Line of
Scottish
retreat

Parliamentary
troops massing

River Teme

? Scottish forward
position

Parliamentary
troops massi

Aerial view showing Powick Hams and the junction of the rivers Teme and Severn, looking north. Note the meanders of the Teme that provided the Scots with a natural

bastion from which to fire into the flanks of the advancing Parliamentary troops. The position of the 'bridge of boats' is indicated. (Photo: Mike Glyde)

connect with his men and counter the more resigned air of his generals. Two infantry brigades (numbering 2,000 men) and a brigade of Horse under Montgomery had now been sent towards the Teme front, to occupy the high ground on Wick Field and line the hedges behind the Teme. A further brigade of Horse and Foot under Major-General Thomas Dalziel (1599–1685) was held back behind them as a final reserve on the road to St John's. Powick Bridge was ordered to be held at all costs, but at this stage it seems that Charles and his generals still believed that this was a diversion, with the main attack to come from the east, following the softening up from the earlier artillery barrage. Only a small percentage (around one-fifth) of the Scottish troops were therefore committed to the west part of the battlefront.

Despite the approach of Scottish reinforcements, Fleetwood's men were busily constructing their bridges of boats at the confluence of the two rivers: one across the 35m-wide Teme and the other some 45m to the north on the 80m-wide Severn (its location described by Sir Nicholas Lechmere as being 'a little above Teme's mouth').[9] This was probably on the site of

The junction of the rivers Teme and Severn. Pontoon bridges were thrown across both rivers during the battle. Interestingly, the defence plan for 1940 anticipated that any Nazi invader would try to cross at the same points. (With thanks to Mick Wilks, pers. comm.)

The location of the 'bridge of boats' across the Teme, looking towards Worcester Cathedral, where Charles II had his look-out.

the ford adjacent to the Ketch. They were built within pistol shot of each other, so that they could provide mutual support. The soldiers were reported to have completed the work in just half an hour, meeting little opposition from the Scots still assembling in the fields on the far bank. A 'forlorn hope' was established on the enemy end of each bridge to protect the work and keep back the enemy with musket fire, supported by covering fire from the opposite bank of the Teme – but they were unable to open up a wider bridgehead as more Scots arrived. This was despite the assistance of Parliamentary artillery, whose cannon balls have been found in the meadows to the east of Manor Farm. It may be presumed that the Scots kept just out of range of the withering musket fire that the massed Parliamentary troops would have been capable of laying down, with the bulk of Montgomery's men still uncommitted to the battle on the riverbank – after all, the Highlanders of Keith and Pitscottie seemed to be successful in holding off the numerically superior Parliamentary forces. One disadvantage may have been that the Parliamentarians had little support

The present banks of the River Teme. The seventeenth-century ground level may have been as much as a metre below the present ground surface.

from their Horse at this stage of the battle, with most of Fleetwood's cavalry being based with the west column, impatiently waiting for an opportunity to cross over Powick and Bransford Bridges. The shoulder of high ground beside Manor Farm probably provided the Scots with a convenient command post overlooking the floodplain, but they found it impossible to regain any initiative.

By 3pm, and following an hour-long exchange of fire, the battle had become bogged down with neither side able to dislodge the other from the banks of the Teme. Including the troops stationed on the hills to the east of Worcester, the battlefront now stretched over a total distance of some 8 miles. A frustrated Cromwell was probably observing the battle from the high ground above the east bank of the Severn at Timberdine and now took decisive action to end the stalemate. He is reported to have personally led his reserve of three crack brigades of New Model Horse and Foot down the steep slope from the high ground on what is now the A38 in Timberdine,

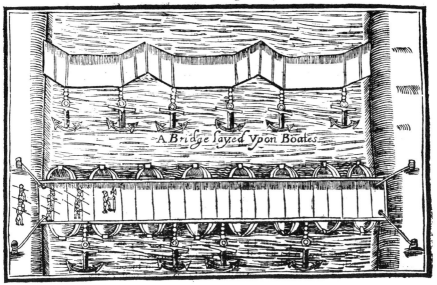

Contemporary illustration of a 'bridge of boats'. From Robert Ward's Animadversions *of Warre (1639). (By courtesy of Brown University Library)*

beside the Ketch public house. In doing so, they probably took advantage of the shallower slope of a natural ravine about 180m to the north of the confluence to reach the riverbank. With few cavalry to oppose them on the floodplain, Cromwell's Horse then stormed across the pontoon bridge over the Severn, punching a hole in the flank of the Scots infantry facing the Teme big enough to allow the Foot to follow and then break out of the narrow bridgeheads in front of the pontoon bridges. Following the initial cavalry charge, the Foot regiments of Fairfax, Goffe and Deane from Cromwell's reserve crossed over the Severn pontoon bridge to take up their own positions in the hedgerows and secure the expanding bridgehead. This was followed by a crossing of the Teme pontoon bridge by the regiments of Blake, Gibbon and Marsh from Fleetwood's column, with Lord Grey's regiment forming the rearguard. Initially there would have been a crush as the troops fought to escape the constraints of the narrow fields adjacent to the Teme. As the infantry regiments fanned out across the meadows, there was fierce fighting for another half an hour, taking the battle to about 3.30pm. The Scots again took advantage of the natural cover and 'lined their hedges thick with men', but the numbers and firepower of the Parliamentarians began to take their toll, with Pitscottie's Highlanders – including MacLeods, MacNeils and Gunns – being steadily pushed back into Montgomery's troops on the high ground beside Manor Farm. The fighting was again described as being by 'push of pike' (a euphemism for hand-to-hand fighting), and from hedge to hedge.[10] The repeated hedge and ditch lines in the enclosed landscape of small fields and meadows were important allies for the out-gunned Scots. To stand back and trade shots with the superior firepower of the Parliamentary troops in a classic Civil War battle would have been to invite annihilation. By contrast, the Parliamentary preference was probably to form up in regular formation and pour the fire of rank after rank into the hedgerows and the Scots hiding behind them, culminating in a massed salvee of all muskets before charging the field gates or cutting their way through the hedges. The logistics of resupplying the troops with powder, ball and match were to be critical during the battle. Each musketeer would carry a bandolier containing just twelve charges of gunpowder, along with a dozen musket-balls and a length of slow-burning match. The Parliamentary side had the resources to peel off units of men for them to be resupplied, refilling their powder bottles from barrels kept towards the rear. They would also have reels of match and barrels of musket-balls ready to hand. The whole effort of the Council of State across the country over the past weeks had been directed towards ensuring that they were well supplied for this day. Yet the Scots could only rely on what they had brought into Worcester or the limited product of the local powder mill.

As the Scottish line was slowly rolled back from the Teme, field boundary by field boundary, Colonel Haines was able to get some of his militia regiment of Foot across the river about a mile to the west of Powick Bridge, opposite Upper Wick. Here he found shallows where it was possible for troops to wade across the Teme. Keith's men at the bridge were now outflanked on both sides and had to give way, allowing the rest of Haines's regiment and Cobbett's newly raised New Model Army regiment (with Matthew's regiment in reserve) to finally force the crossing over Powick Bridge. Keith himself was captured in the fighting. With Powick Bridge now in his hands and temporarily repaired, the frustrated Fleetwood could at last move his Foot and Horse over the Teme in substantial numbers and start to advance up the 1.3 miles (2,100m) through the fields of Lower Wick into St John's and thence to Worcester. At the same time Dragoons forced the crossing at Bransford

Bridge, allowing over Fleetwood's and Twistleton's regiments of Horse and Kendrick's Dragoons. Their first task was to cut off any troops attempting to escape north into Herefordshire or Shropshire. Some of the survivors of Keith's brigade may have reached as far as Cotheridge (3.5 miles) before they were finally cut down. The Parliamentary Horse and Dragoons then swung round to advance back down the road towards St John's and the main river crossing into Worcester. Parliamentary troops were now crossing the Teme at three points. Fleetwood's cavalry brigade picked its way through the hedges and ditches of the enclosed fields and swept down the lanes, both cutting off any possibility of escape westwards and driving any Scots attempting to escape back towards Worcester itself. At the same time the troops coming up from Powick passed by the late medieval manor complex of the present-day Manor Farm. As Montgomery's brigade continued to fall back towards St John's it finally ran out of ammunition and Montgomery himself was seriously wounded. The cavalry would aim to break up enemy formations, turning the Scottish retreat into a rout and making them easy targets for the musketeers. Here the flexibility of the dragoons would be particularly useful, as they were able to quickly outflank the retreating enemy, then dismount to engage as musketeers before riding on again. The survivors were pushed back into the final reserve of Dalziel's brigade, trying to

View from the tower of Worcester Cathedral, looking south-west towards Powick. The landscape still gives an impression of the network of hedged fields of 1651. Charles II had his first glimpse of the battle from this position.

St John's

Outer defences to bridge

Location o[f] medieval bridge

View from the tower of Worcester Cathedral, looking north-west towards St John's. The Scots on the west bank of the Severn made their last stand here on the afternoon of 3 September.

hold the hamlet of St John's and maintain control of the road junction against the threat of attack from both south and west. Two heroes of the retreat were Lieutenant-Colonel Shaw of Dunfermline's Horse and Norman MacLeod of Berneray, who were both knighted in the field for their efforts in slowing the Parliamentary advance. Dalziel's brigade does not appear to have provided significant support to the troops fighting their way back from the Teme. But with the enemy Horse advancing from Bransford it is likely that the Scots were unwilling to attempt any serious counter-attack towards the Teme with their reserve as this would leave them exposed to the risk of being cut off from Worcester and surrounded.

Thus Cromwell declared, 'We beat the enemy from hedge to hedge, till we beat him into Worcester'.[11]

By around 4pm the surviving Scots on this side of the river had been pushed out of St John's and down Cripplegate. They probably made their final stand by the triangular bastion defending the Severn bridge, fighting on until around 5pm when Fleetwood finally forced a passage across the bridge (see Chapter Five). After the battle the road into St John's, flanked by hedged fields until the scatter of buildings extending from St John's Green (the present Bransford Road, A4103), was said to be lined with the Scottish dead all along its route. Nineteenth-century tradition reported by Willis Bund tells of burial pits from this action on Powick Hams, and this has been linked to the site of two large hollows in the

Major-General Thomas Dalziel, commander of the Scottish reserve in St John's.

overlying silt, where a former farmer has reported discovering human bones during deep ploughing.[12] If true, the pits may have been on the south bank of the river, adjacent to the bridge of boats, because the responsibility for burial passed to Powick parish. Given the tradition it is, however, surprising that there is no indication of the burials from later field names and the original landform is now deeply buried by post-seventeenth-century river silt.

Although the main force of Scottish cavalry was based just the other side of the river in Pitchcroft, with access through St Clement's Gate to the bridge over the Severn, they made no attempt to relieve their beleaguered comrades, even when the dire nature of the situation became clear for anyone to see or hear. Charles faced a dilemma. Was he to try to relieve his men, or sacrifice them to their fate? He may have decided that

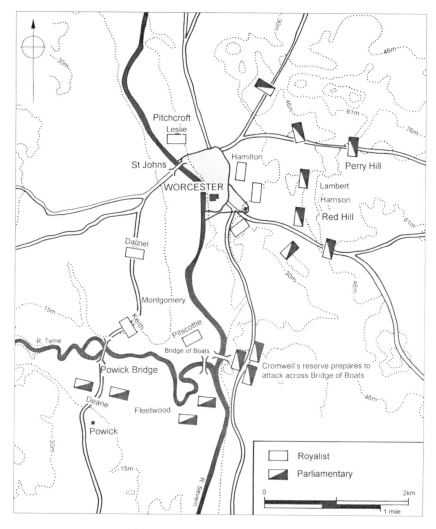

Disposition of troops around 3pm.

the situation was already lost and did not wish to trap more of his men on the west bank and open himself up to the risk of attack from the east side of the river. Leslie may have realised, as Fleetwood had done before him, that the landscape was not suitable for cavalry engagements and

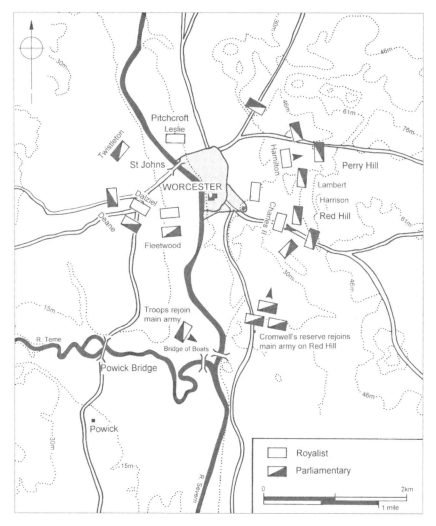

Disposition of troops around 4pm.

that his men would be cut to pieces by the musketeers now massing in Cripplegate. But this was not to be the last time in the battle that Leslie failed to provide support to the rest of the army in times of critical danger.

Chapter Five

Counter-attack and Final Victory

The Lord gave our men to gaine grounde of the enemy, till we had beaten them out of the ground: the charges was very hot for a while, but the Lord owned us in this contest, and the enemy fled before us.[1]

4pm–10pm

As the battle raged on the west bank of the River Severn, the Scottish field hospitals within the city began to fill with the wounded. One hospital was possibly at the Commandery in Sidbury, others would have been in local churches. There were at least nine surgeons attached to the army. Treatment was crude. The causes of infection were only just beginning to be understood and this meant that the simplest means of dealing with a wound in the limb was to amputate. Operations were carried out with the patient in a sitting position and with alcohol as the only form of pain relief. The surgeons, however, preferred to operate while the patient was still conscious – so that if he died he would go to his maker in a fit state! The surgeon Richard Wiseman amputated the arm of one Scot shot in the shoulder during the battle. He urged the soldier to endure the pain but the patient cried out 'give me a drink, and I will die'! Sadly, he did not survive.[2]

By late afternoon, with Parliamentary troops approaching the city through St John's from both the south and the west, King Charles was driven to desperate measures. Cromwell had now committed around half his army (15,000 men) on the west side of the Severn against only a small proportion of the Scottish forces (3,000 men). Charles was probably unaware of the total strength of the Parliamentary forces but by now must have realised that the determined and wide-ranging attack on the west was no mere feint and that soon he would be completely trapped within the walls of the city. There had still been no sign of action from the Parliamentary army on the east side of Worcester, although the artillery barrage against Fort Royal had been renewed. Having seen Cromwell bring his reserve from the east side of the Severn across the bridge of boats, he hoped, however, that those on that side had now been over-weakened. Cromwell's ability to manoeuvre both parts of the army also depended on the single pontoon bridge across the Severn. Edmund Ludlow's account of the battle does indeed claim that Cromwell had tried to further reduce the strength of the forces on the east by ordering Lambert to cross the Severn

View down the slope of 'Cromwell's Trenches', on the north side of Perry Wood, looking west into the city from the position of the Parliamentary artillery battery. The Duke of Hamilton and his troops charged up here during the Royalist counter-attack at 4pm. There have been many reports of lead shot, including possible case-shot from the Parliamentary cannon, being found in this area.

with his cavalry brigade. Lambert is supposed to have refused, protesting that 'if the enemy should alter their course, and fall upon them on this side, they might probably cut off all that remained'.[3] But Ludlow, who was in Ireland at the time, is an unreliable commentator who bitterly opposed Cromwell and the account is not supported by any other contemporary account. Given that the anticipated Royalist response to attack was considered to be an attempt to flee then it seems likely that Cromwell would have weighed the balance of strength required on each side of the river very carefully, and there had already been enough complaints from the Horse about the difficulty of operating in the fields to the west of the Severn.

At around 4pm King Charles decided to launch the pincer movement counter-attack (as discussed with his generals in the morning) against the troops in the centre of the Parliamentary line, sited on the high ground to the east. He may have been aware that the troops on the front line, under

Plan of Fort Royal and the adjacent Civil War defences, from a map of 1795.

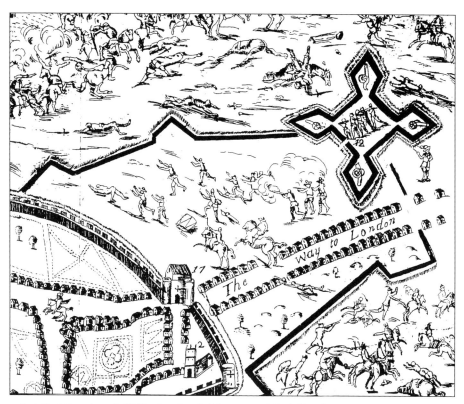

Detail of the plan of 1660, showing fighting around Fort Royal. (By courtesy of Worcester City Library)

the overall command of Cromwell's brother-in-law Major-General John Desborough (1608–80), were raw militia men and therefore a potential weak spot. This bold move may have owed something to the advice of Massie, who had employed the same tactic at Gloucester during the siege of 1643. The King still had 7,000 Foot based in the city and on the land to the east, 3,000 Horse to the north on Pitchcroft, and the small force of English Horse – giving not unreasonable odds compared to the 18,000 or so men of Cromwell's army on that side. A carefully focused assault might even deliver superiority in numbers at the point of attack. His men in St John's might be lost, but the attack might move the course of battle eastwards, providing Charles with the advantage of the high ground on Red Hill and Perry Wood. This may have been the attempt, predicted by

Detail of the plan of 1660, showing Sidbury Gate. (By courtesy of Worcester City Library)

the Council of State and Cromwell before the battle, to punch a hole through the Parliamentary blockade, winning an important psychological victory, and achieve a break-out towards London. The Royalist intelligence was probably not aware of the fact that even if they did by some good fortune break through the Parliamentary lines at Worcester, then further troops were waiting for them in the Midlands, with another 15,000 in London (equivalent alone to his total strength) against just such an eventuality.

Cromwell and other commentators believed that the King had drawn out all the troops remaining within the city to take part in the attack, convincing them that this was an all-or-nothing venture.[4] General Sir John Middleton (later joined by the Duke of Hamilton) led the north arm of the pincer out of St Martin's Gate, with Charles himself leading the charge out of Sidbury Gate and the outer defences beside Fort Royal. A reserve was held back between the two in the marshy area of the 'blockhouse'. The men and artillery in Fort Royal would provide covering fire. The forces consisted of mixed Highland and Lowland Foot, including the regiment of Sir Alexander Forbes, supported by the small force of English Horse under the Duke of Buckingham and Lord Grandison. But of critical importance to the course of events, the 3,000 men of Leslie's Horse did not take part in the attack. The immediate purpose was to encircle and destroy the enemy positions at the centre of their line on Red Hill and Perry Wood. The attacking troops would have been covered initially by the cannon mounted at Fort Royal but then faced the difficult task of charging uphill against an enemy that was well dug-in and well supplied with ammunition. The contemporary landscape still survives at the point where the Duke of Hamilton charged the north side of Perry Wood. His Horse and Foot had to pick their way uphill across the corrugated landscape of medieval ridge and furrow, with Parliamentary musketeers delivering fire from both flanks, from the woods and from the sides of former quarries.[5] None the less the ferocity of the attack appeared to have taken the Parliamentary forces by surprise: some troops did reach

The fourteenth-century Edgar Gate, leading into the College Green. This gives an impression of what the gates to the city defences may have looked like.

the ridge and fought for possession of the guns, with the fighting spreading out into the adjacent woodland. Charles's attack on Red Hill against Croxton's Cheshire militia also met initial success, despite the heavy gunfire coming from beside London Road on Red Hill and Green Hill. Charles was praised for leading the charge in person, supported especially by the ferocious Highlanders. Some cannon were overrun but, like Middleton and Hamilton to the north, he was unable to exploit this temporary advantage.

Despite such initial success, if Charles actually believed that the Parliamentary line had been seriously depleted he was to receive a rude shock. With the battle seemingly on a knife's edge, the three regiments of the Essex militia (under Sir Thomas Honywood, Joachim Matthews and Thomas Cooke) held the line on Perry Hill and Red Hill. The Essex men had been so disturbed by the sound of their own cannon in the barrage the day before that they had thrown themselves to the ground 'so amazed at the shot of the cannon, that some of them fell flat on their faces'.[6] But now, although the line fell back, it did not break, stiffened by the New Model Army regiments of Pride and Cooper, while behind them the second line of the New Model Army regiments, including Desborough's Horse, quickly moved up to support them. Essex and Surrey militia Horse and Dragoons may also have been engaged here. It is likely that the final reserves in the rear were the 'country people' that had recently joined the army in the tradition of the *posse comitatus*.

With the support of Leslie's Horse the outcome to this counter-attack might have been different. At the point at which the Parliamentary line appeared to be on the point of collapse a determined cavalry charge may just have broken through to create disorder behind them, but the Scottish Horse remained stationary on Pitchcroft and around St Martin's Gate. Either Leslie was now convinced that the day was lost and was only looking for an opportunity to escape with his men (as later detractors accused), or he was waiting for an opportunity to charge and turn the Parliamentary flank. He may well have feared that any movement from his position to support Middleton and the King would bring down a charge of the main Parliamentary Horse that was shadowing him. But the landscape of ditches and watercourses around the 'blockhouse' outside the city walls was as unwelcoming to cavalry as the hedges to the south of the city. For their part the main body of Parliamentary Horse also made no attempt at this stage to turn from their principal task and support their embattled Foot to the south. Leslie was certainly depressed and confused throughout the day, a far cry from the shrewd and decisive cavalry commander of the battle of Marston Moor or even the strategist of the early months of the campaign in 1650. He may simply have been incapable of making a decision at that time. Charles seemed to have discounted the later accusations of cowardice and, despite his more general disparaging comments towards the Scottish army, elevated Leslie to Baron Newark after the Restoration. But such a debate was irrelevant to the English Royalists and Scottish Covenanters who were now in desperate straits on the brow of the hills, again outnumbered and fast running out of ammunition. With empty powder-flasks and no musket-balls, the Highland and Lowland Foot were forced to fight on using the butt ends of their muskets as clubs. Casualties mounted: Royalist commanders were clearly leading from the front to try to drive their men on. The Duke of Hamilton and Middleton were both wounded, Hamilton fatally from a 'slug shot', with his horse killed under him. His deathbed letter to his wife began thus:

> Dear Heart,
> You know I have long been labouring, though in great weakness to be prepared against this expected change, and I thank my God I find comfort in it, in this my day of tryal; for my body is not more weakened by my wounds, than I find my spirit comforted and supported by the infinite mercies and great love of my Blessed redeemer, who will be with me to the end and in the end . . . [7]

Try as they might, the Scots could not exploit their initial success and as the attack lost its momentum the problem then arose as to how to extricate themselves and once again gain the comparative safety of the city walls.

Some of the Royalist Horse on Perry Hill tried to escape into the woods; here the wounded Sir Alexander Forbes, shot in both calves, was found the next day.

The Parliamentary side evidently had excellent battlefield communications across the whole 8-mile front. Cromwell, upon hearing of the attack, quickly brought his reserve of Horse back from the west side of the river across the bridge of boats on the Severn, and skirted the Scottish defences to join the main army to the north of the London Road. Nothing shows Cromwell's tactical awareness and self-assuredness to greater effect as he moved large bodies of troops back and forth across the Worcester battlefield, completely changing the direction of the action to his own advantage. This is in sharp contrast to the indecision displayed on the Royalist side. Led by Hacker's Horse, Cromwell's reserves then threw themselves into action in support of the troops on Red Hill and Perry Wood. This may have been where the commander of Cromwell's Lifeguard, Captain Howard, was wounded as he 'did interpose very seasonably and happily at a place of much danger, where he gave the

The present site of Sidbury Gate, with the Commandery behind.

enemy (though with his personal smarts) a severe check when our foot, for want of horse, were hard put to it'.[8] If so, Howard's comment confirms that the cavalry brigades of Lambert and Harrison had remained on their station to the north, facing Leslie's Horse.

Despite the frantic personal urgings of King Charles, the Scots were forced to give way, falling back to Fort Royal, with Cromwell now pouring 'reserve upon reserve' into the fray.[9] Thomas Blount's *Boscobel* particularly bemoans the fact that they did not have their own cavalry to repel the attacks of the Parliamentary Horse. Charles is reported as commanding the rearguard to protect the retreat of his men, then trying to order a last counter-attack standing on the earth ramparts of Fort Royal. There was indeed a brief local rally, pushing back Parliamentary troops with some loss before the Scottish advance again ground to a halt. It proved impossible to regroup the men on any scale, their ranks torn apart by the Parliamentary musket and cannon fire and they now swept back past the King in disorder. On a fresh mount Charles had to be dragged back into the city 'at about the shutting in of the evening' by his aides to avoid being killed or captured. When he reached Sidbury Gate he was obliged to dismount and scramble over the hastily erected barricades. In a gruesome incident in this phase of the battle a Scottish musketeer in Fort Royal was attempting to refill his bandolier from a resupply of powder that he had scooped up into his bonnet. While he was kneeling on the ground to do this a second musketeer came up and, not realising what was happening, stood over the first man and fired his weapon at the enemy. A spark from his pan ignited the powder below and both men suffered horrific powder burns.

> A Souldier in the time of service being in the Fort-Royal at Worcester, hastily fetched his bonnet full of Gun-powder; and whilest he was filling his Bandeliers, another Souldier carelessly bestrides it, to make a Shot at one of the Enemies which he saw lying perdue. In firing his Musket, a spark flew out of the Pan, and gave fire to the Powder underneath him, and grievously burned the Hands, Arms, Breast, Neck and Face of him that was filling his Bandeliers. And as to himself, he likewise was burned and scorched in all the upper part of his Thighs, Scrotum, the Muscles of the Abdomen, and the Coats of the Testicles to the Erythroides, so that the Cremasters were visible. And indeed it was to be feared, that, when the Eschar should cast off from his Belly, his Bowells would have tumbled out.[10]

The failure of this desperate gamble by King Charles had now given Cromwell a new advantage. Having taken a large percentage of his remaining troops outside the protection of the Worcester defences, and with their formations now in a disorderly retreat, Charles had fatally exposed his men. If Cromwell could attack now, whatever his original battle plan may have been for the day, he might avoid a prolonged and costly siege. This was no time for hesitation. It is therefore likely that at this stage Cromwell ordered Lambert and Harrison on the east and Fleetwood on the west to use any opportunity to enter the city. The success of this gamble, sparing the likely human and financial costs of a protracted siege, was to be described as 'a very glorious mercy' by Cromwell.[11]

Seizing the initiative, following an hour of bitter fighting on the slopes of Red Hill and around Perry Wood, at around 5pm Cromwell gave his men on the heights above Worcester the order to fall upon the enemy. Cromwell used the militia Foot as the first assault wave, conserving the regiments of the New Model Army. As the drums beat out the insistent call of 'Battle', a ferocious roar of 'The Lord of Hosts' can be imagined as the Essex militia swept down from their positions. Cooke's regiment took the honour of storming Fort Royal 'to the very mouth of their cannons'. There was a real blood-lust in this part of the engagement that fulfilled the threat of their war cry. This is what the Essex men had rushed to Worcester for, encapsulating the wider frustrations of the country about the new outbreak of war and the invasion of their country by the Scots. The militia would have fired one last volley or salvee and then swung their muskets around, holding them by the hot barrels and wielding them as crude but devastating clubs. Cooke's men then charged, scrambling across the ditch and over the ramparts of Fort Royal; they massacred its terrified defenders, taking no prisoners. They 'put all the Scots they found therein to the sword'.[12] King Charles did, indeed, have a narrow escape. As the blue and white Scottish saltire was torn down and replaced by the new blue flag of the Commonwealth with its St George's Cross and Irish harp, the impact of this capture would have been evident to the rest of the Scots in the city. At this point it appears that Cromwell sent a messenger to offer one last chance to surrender (other versions say that it was Cromwell himself who delivered the message but this seems unlikely). Against the etiquette of contemporary warfare the Scots shot at the messenger – an action that was hardly likely to endear them to their assailants![13] The capture of Fort Royal divided the Scottish troops who were outside the main city defences and allowed access through the outer defences to the road into Worcester. The defensive 'seal' had been broken. The Essex militia now reformed and turned their attention to the main body of the Scots Foot who had been drawn up on the land north of Fort Royal. These were now outflanked and trapped outside the city walls. Their only escape would be through

St Martin's Gate, but as they retreated the militia attacked to take as many as possible in the open. Up to 1,500 men were reported to have been killed in this part of the battle, and although the exact numbers might be questionable this was undoubtedly the most savage episode of fighting. Stapleton also says that the army took few prisoners before the troops entered the city. The Parliamentary troops did not, however, attempt to storm St Martin's Gate as it was probably protected by the Scottish Horse and remained in Scottish hands for the rest of the battle (with great significance for the later escape of Charles II). The Scottish Horse had, however, now lost the supporting fire of the Foot lying dead and wounded against the city walls, and it put them at an enormous disadvantage for any future action.

The Scottish cannon on Fort Royal, probably reinforced with Parliamentary field guns, were turned upon the city and the rest of the Scots from King Charles's column, who were now desperately trying to retreat down the south side of the Fort Royal defences and along London Road towards Sidbury Gate.[14] Case-shot would have poured hundreds of musket-sized balls into the backs of the fleeing Scots. The gate was an impressive structure, three storeys high and with a wide entrance way. Considered an internal gate by virtue of the outer defences around Fort Royal, it had been closed only by an ammunition wagon overturned across its carriageway. A local carter, John Moore from Elmley Lovett, who had probably been impressed into Royalist service, was later to claim credit for this but he was more likely simply acting under instruction for what was a standard, and now urgent, means of defence. In any case the cart was forced aside by the crush of Scots trying to escape the fury of the battle around Fort Royal. Close on their heels charged Major Swallow's troop from Whalley's regiment of Horse. Swallow was the former commander of the famous 'Maiden Troop' of Cromwell's original Ironsides, raised from Norwich. Swallow's men rode down the Scots, slashing at them with their swords and trampling them underfoot, and seized the gate. This in turn allowed the Foot of the Cheshire militia and further cavalry from Harrison's Horse, who were now also advancing down London Road, to pour through the gate and fan out through the streets and alleyways into the city. With the inner defences breached, the Scottish forces dispersed and their command structure disintegrating, Worcester was now lost. As the light failed, Baxter described how the Scots were 'trodden down and slain in the streets'. For those who believed in the divine right of kings, the events seemed to go against nature itself as 'the Dusk of which Fatall Evening, when the ashamed Sun had blush't in his setting, and plunged his afrighted Head into the depth of the Lucklesse Severn'. For the

Parliamentarian Robert Stapleton, however, the setting of the sun was more symbolic of the setting of Royalist fortunes as 'this was the beginning of their fall before the appearance of the Lord Jesus, this seems to be the setting of the young king's glory'.[15] A Scottish cavalry officer, not unbiased, claimed that the Foot 'in disorder threw downe their arms', while the Horse still 'disputed it from street to street'. Even in defeat the Scottish army was divided and full of self-reproach.[16] At the same time Dalziel's reserve in St John's finally collapsed and surrendered under the onslaught of Fleetwood's men, although the wounded Montgomery managed to escape back into Worcester. The drawbridge into the city had been left intact to allow free movement of the Scottish army and Fleetwood's men managed to force a passage across the drawbridge before it could be raised and so entered the city. This was probably another unexpected

Detail from an engraving of 1764, showing the medieval bridge over the Severn. In 1651 it was just inside the line of the north defences of the city and adjacent to St Clement's church. Fleetwood's men stormed the bridge at about 5pm and entered the city.

development but meant that Fleetwood's Horse could now charge into the city from the west along Broad Street and High Street, linking up with Whalley's and Harrison's Horse who were entering from the east.

If this was not bad enough for the Scots, Cromwell had also ordered part of the army on the west side of the Severn, their job now done, to cross to the east and make a breach through the south defences of the city. This was to ensure that decisive force would be used to guarantee the success of the storming of the city. The footsore and weary troops – who had marched 9 miles and then fought a battle of over three hours – passed over the bridge of boats, up through Diglis and attacked the defences along Severn Street, below the castle. This was to be the only frontal assault on the defences of the city. Despite fire from the castle, the troops, including the 1,000 men of Cobbett's Foot, raised only in the previous month, managed to cross the 10m-wide ditches, some 2.4m deep and with a steep earth rampart on the inner side. From there they contained the troops now trapped on the castle mound and swept further into the city. With troops now pouring into the city from three directions and more men still coming down from the high ground of Red Hill and Perry Wood, Charles desperately tried to order one last rally from his Horse , to 'scour' the enemy from outside the city walls and try to isolate the Parliamentary troops within. By now exhausted from the heat of battle, he stripped off his armour in Friar Street, leaving his thick buff coat, and took a fresh horse. Again he desperately tried to rally both Foot and Horse, going again 'hat in his hand' to beg them to 'stand to their arms and fight like men'. But his men 'were so confused that neither threats nor entreaty would persuade them to charge with His Majesty'.[17] The noise of fighting would now have been echoing from all sides, the flames from the gun muzzles flashing through the sky and the smoke hanging heavily in the narrow streets. This was now the last quarter of the city in Royalist hands. Leslie was described as riding 'up and down as one amazed or seeking to fly', while his men 'trampling one upon another, [were] much readier to cut each other's throats than to defend ourselves against the enemy'.[18] The King's army had disintegrated as an organised fighting force. As the fighting raged through the streets and into the houses, some troops may have been able to take advantage of Massie's firepikes, spitting burning tar from leather jacks tied to the ends of pikes to turn horses aside, but it was to be of no avail. Cromwell had by now committed his entire army to assault the city which 'fell to storming without any reserve'.[19] The death toll among the Scots would have been higher had not many of the Parliamentary troops quickly lost interest in the fighting to concentrate on looting the city! One Scottish officer had a lucky escape. The 27-year-old Sir

Andrew Melvill was dragged from his horse in the final stages of the battle and was about to be stripped of his clothing by soldiers when an officer tried to claim him as his own prize. Resenting this, one of the soldiers simply shot Melvill in the stomach in order to spoil the clothing and spite the officer. Melvill was left to die but in the morning was found by a Parliamentary officer who took pity on him and had him taken into a nearby house to be cared for. This house was then looted by more Parliamentary soldiers who even took the bed on which Melvill was sleeping. He was dragged from the house and left to die in a ditch, with a corpse casually thrown on top of him. Fortunately the widow who owned the house and her daughters rescued him and treated his wounds over the next three months until he was able to travel in hiding to London and thence to the continent. Despite all this, and subsequent wounds suffered as a mercenary on the continent, Sir Andrew reached the ripe old age of 82.

Having again failed to rally the Scottish Horse, a depressed King Charles managed to retreat to his quarters on the Cornmarket before it was reached by the Parliamentary troops, declaring 'I had rather you would shoot me, than keep me alive to see the sad consequences of this day'.[20] An assessment of the King's part in the battle was written soon after the events by an imprisoned Scottish officer but his tale was then heavily edited in the

Reconstruction of the profile of the Civil War defences on Severn Street. (By courtesy of Worcestershire Historic Environment and Archaeology Service)

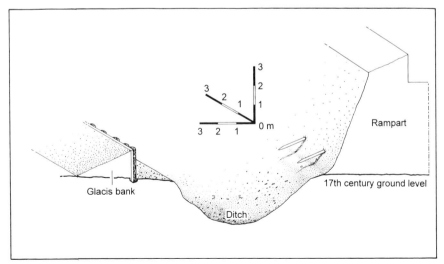

The surviving city wall on City Walls Road. The line of the ditch ran along the line of the modern road.

Royal Court. It could be dismissed as sycophancy and the start of the royal legend of the battle, but it has the ring of truth as Charles desperately tried to motivate an army that was falling apart around him: 'certainly a braver prince never lived; having in the day of the fight hazarded his person much more than any officer of his army, riding from regiment to regiment'.[21] He felt bitterly let down by the Scots, claiming that only 5,000 had fought as they should.[22] But putting pride and bravado aside, he had to plan an escape – and quickly. The small contingent of English Royalists bought him valuable time by mounting two diversionary charges away from him, along Sidbury Street and High Street. Led by the Earl of Cleveland, Sir James Hamilton and Colonel Carlis, Lord Talbot's troop of Midlands Royalists formed the core of the attack. The Parliamentary troops now looting the city were initially unprepared for this unexpected offensive. After the initial shock, however, the Royalists took heavy casualties. They had, though, succeeded in their aim, delaying by valuable minutes the arrival of London dragoons sent to capture the King. The dragoons reputedly broke down the front door of the house as Charles left by the rear, hurrying to escape via St Martin's Gate. In his haste he left behind his collar of All Saints and the Garter. By now St Martin's was the only gate in Scottish hands, protected by the bulk of the much-derided Scottish Horse, and Charles was lost in the crowd of cavalry and gentry trying to flee. The failure to seal this gate, overlooked in the sudden change in the direction of the battle in the early evening, was the only flaw in Cromwell's battle plan and was to have momentous consequences. When the Scottish Horse, with the King in their midst, tried to make their break for freedom, the remainder of the Parliamentary Horse that had been observing them from the heights of Elbury Hill (and had not joined in the storm of the city) set off to harry them. Further reinforcements followed over the next hours as the Horse were reformed once their bloody work inside the city was completed. Whalley's Horse was quickly on the scene,

The city wall and St Martin's Tower, City Walls Road.

Aerial view showing the landscape from Fort Royal (bottom right) into the city, looking west. (Photo: Mike Glyde)

Mealcheapen Street. At about 6pm Parliamentary troops detached from a London regiment of dragoons charged down here to try to capture the King.

Broad Street. Fleetwood's cavalry charged down here after crossing the bridge over the River Severn.

and was said to have pursued both Foot and Horse out of the North Gate.[23] Colonel Blundell left with 1,500 Horse before dawn of the next day, with Harrison following on with the rest of his brigade in the morning. Cromwell was content to let Harrison and the forces he had placed for such an eventuality along the anticipated line of retreat mop up these men, while he focused on what to do with the bulk of the army that was captured within Worcester.

As their King fled, at around 6pm, the majority of the Foot were relentlessly pushed back to the quay wall (the area behind the Technical College around the present Copenhagen Street car park) where most eventually surrendered. Most of the fighting was over by 8pm (according to Colonel Robert Stapleton) as darkness fell, but the English in the army could have expected little mercy and a small group made a last stand in the Town Hall (the site of the modern Guildhall on the High Street) until killed or captured. The final fighting took place around the castle mound where 1,300 men under John Leslie, Earl of Rothes (1630–81), and Colonel William Drummond (1617–88) managed to hold out until about 10pm. Some may have remained in hiding until later: Royalist accounts maintain that Colonel Wogan managed to break out of the city around midnight with about 50 horse, to follow the route taken by the King.

In all the battle had lasted ten hours, the latter stages being described by Cromwell as 'as stiffe a contest for four or five houres as ever I have seen'. He reserved especial praise for the militias who 'did perform singular good service'.[24] The militia Foot were in the front line of the battle and their Dragoons played a key role in the advance west of the

Severn. Casualty figures among the Scots vary widely from 2,000 to 4,000. By contrast, Parliamentary losses were put at only 100–200. Given the ferocity of the fighting, much of it hand-to-hand, and the immense firepower rained down upon the Scots, it is perhaps surprising that the death toll was not higher.

The search for Royalists and the widespread looting of the city continued well into 4 September. Colonel Stapleton, for one, decided not to enter the city until 'the soldiers fury was over'. Cromwell's men

A medieval merchant's house next to the Greyfriars on Friar Street. This was the last part of the city under Royalist control when Charles decided to make his escape. It would have been the scene of bitter street fighting.

showed little mercy as 'Lords, knights and gentlemen were there plucked out of holes by the soldiers'. All across the city doors would have been kicked in, homes searched, possessions looted and trampled. Any householder's protestations of loyalty to Parliament would have made little difference.[25] No distinction could be made in the heat of the moment between possible Parliamentary or Royalist sympathisers. Cromwell was forced to write to Parliament that supporters in the town suffered alongside the Royalists: 'The town being entered by storm, some honest men, promiscuously and without distinction, suffered by your Soldier – which could not at that time possibly be prevented, in the fury and heat of the battle.'[26] Stolen goods included the Civic Sword. A new sword had to be purchased in 1652 at a cost of £5 8s 6d,[27] and 5s even had to be paid to a soldier to return some civic records to the Treasury. Wine glasses, bottles, butter pots and pewter dishes were all lost from the Deanery. Nicholas Lechmere of Hanley Castle wrote in his diary, 'The city of Worcester was taken by storm and all the wealth in it became booty to the soldier'. Sir Rowland Berkeley of Cotheridge wrote of 'all houses being ransacked from top to bottom, the very persons of men and women not excepted, and the ruin of many families'. This brutal treatment was the prize for troops forced to storm a town's defences, and a dread warning for any other place that decided to shelter the enemies of the state. The consequences may, however, have been even more dire if the events of 3 September had dragged on into a siege and any formal demand to surrender had been refused. The lives of the soldiers, at least, would then have become forfeit, as Cromwell had demonstrated at Drogheda in Ireland in 1649.

The city later estimated the total cost of plundering after the battle at £80,000 and some of the debts were not repaid until 1675. The Scottish army was accompanied by a number of civilian camp followers. Some of the men had brought their wives and families with them (there being no other means of support for them at home). History is silent as to their fate but for them that night must have been a fearful one, separated from their loved ones, not knowing if the latter were dead or alive, and subject to the whims of a vengeful army and civilian population. Sir Thomas Urquart of Cromarty, aged 40, was one of the Royalist camp followers billeted in All Saints parish. He complained bitterly that his possessions were 'plundered, pillaged, pilfered, robbed and rifled' after the battle. He had brought with him four large trunks of clothes including scarlet cloaks and buff suits and also three trunks containing his precious writings. The house was ransacked, his clothes stolen and his manuscripts at first scattered and then used to wrap food, light tobacco pipes and, worst of all to Urquart, used for 'posterior purposes'. A few of his possessions were eventually recovered from under a pile of twenty-seven corpses in a Worcester street.[28]

Dawn would have revealed a terrible sight. Sir Rowland Berkeley described an horrific scene of dead bodies lying from Powick Bridge into St John's, and in almost every street of the city.[29] Corpses lay within houses, in the College and Cathedral, in the cloisters and in Cathedral Green, and on the east side of the city for a mile beyond Sidbury on the land from Fort Royal on to Red Hill. With civic organisation in a state of collapse, the rotting bodies of men and horses were still there three days after the battle so that 'with the dead bodies of men and the dead horses of the enemy filling the streets, there was such a nastiness that a man could hardly abide the town'.[30] It may be for that reason that Cromwell seems to have quickly decided to re-establish his headquarters at Evesham before returning in triumph to London. It would have fallen to the citizens of Worcester to bury the dead, unknown and stripped of their clothes and possessions. Much of this work was done by the parishioners of St Michael Bedwardine. The parish included the area in front of the Cathedral, the Bishop's Palace and down to the river frontage, scenes of some of the most bitter fighting in the closing stages of the battle and where many of the Scots finally surrendered. The parishioners provided a litter at a cost of 6d to carry away the dead and dying, as well as burying them in their churchyard at a cost of £2 9s 4d.[31] Some of the dead were also buried in the Cathedral churchyard; others were reputed by later tradition to have been buried in large pits on Powick Ham. A skeleton was also found in the city ditch beside Nash's Passage in 1975, which was thought at the time to be possibly from the Civil War.[32] Nevertheless there is a marked lack of references to the burial of the dead in the local records, the compilation of which was greatly disrupted throughout the period.

Cromwell's victory at Worcester brought the Civil Wars to a close. The relief was felt by all. For Cromwell, 'The dimensions of this mercy are above my thoughts. It is, for aught I know, a crowning mercy.'[33] On a personal note, this was to be the last time that he personally took to the field. The chaplain Hugh Peters gave a rousing sermon for the assembled troops on the day after the battle, before the militia were dismissed back to their homes. In Shakespearean tones, they were instructed to say 'when their wives and children should ask them where they had been and what news, they should say they had been at Worcester, where England's sorrows began, and where they were happily ended'.[34] They knew that they had taken part in a decisive piece of history. Theirs had been a religious crusade and they were to go home 'their faces shining, having spoken with Him on the Mount'. They were 'the monuments of mercy' but were not to go home boasting 'but humble and wondering'. On a more earthly level the men were also told to think well of the army and the government for having led them to victory.

Chapter Six

Flight and Capture

In the night we kept close together, yet some fell asleep on their horses, and if their horses tarried behind, we might hear by their cries what the bloody country people were doing with them.[1]

Around 10,000 prisoners, mainly Foot, were captured within Worcester. The Scottish Horse, not trapped within the city walls, fled en masse – fulfilling the fears expressed by the Foot before the battle that they would be deserted. Many of the senior officers, excepting those who were seriously wounded, also fled. Even the surgeon Richard Wiseman deserted his patients. Most of the escapees were, however, rounded up over the coming days.

The common footsoldiers had no such opportunity to flee and had to throw themselves on the mercy of their captors. The prisoners taken in the city were divided according to rank, with most being driven into the Cathedral as the largest building in the city, and thus capable of containing such a large number of men. Others were herded into the Town Hall (Guildhall) which incorporated a large hall that in happier times had been used as a tennis court but which had to be disinfected after the battle at a cost of '2s – Paid for stonpitch and rosen to perfume the hall after the Scots'.[2] Cooper's regiment of Foot provided one of the guard units. Many of the prisoners would have been wounded

King Charles House on New Street. This building had served as the King's quarters during the battle, and it was from here that he made his escape in the early evening.

117

FROM THE ACCOUNT OF COLONEL ROBERT STAPLETON

An exact List of the Prisoners taken.

Earle of *Darby*.
Earle of *Cleaveland*.
Earle of *Shrewesbury*.
Duke *Hamylton*.
Earle *Louderdale*.
Earle of *Rothis*.
Earle of *Cornwagh*.
Earle of *Kellsey*.
Lord *Sinclare*.
Sir *John Packington*.
Lord *Spyne*.
Sir *Charles Cunningham*.
Sir *Ralph Clare*.
Collonell *Graves*.
Mr *Richard Fanshaw*, the King of *Scots* Secretary.

Collonels of Horse:
Col. *William Hurry*.
Col. *William Kent*.
Col. *John Cheston*.
Col. *Benbow*.
Col. *Gibt Cambel*.
Col. *John Forbs*.
Col. Sir. *David Ogleby*.
Col. *Geor. Montgomery*.
Col. *John Shaw*.
Col. *James Ogleby*.

13 Collonels of Foot, whereof 3 are Reformades.

Col. S. *James Graham*.
Col. Sir *Tho. Orquaint*.
Col. *John Butler*.
Col. *Tho. Thomson*.
Col. Sir *Thomas Hume*.

9 Lieut. Collonels of Horse, whereof one a Reformade.
8 Lieut. Collonels of Foot.
8 Majors of Horse.
13 Majors of Foot.
37 Captaines of Horse.
72 Captaines of Foot, whereof 8 are Reformades.
55 Quarter Masters of Horse.
84 Lieut. of Foot.

Generall Officers:
Ma. Generall *Pitscotty*.
Ma. Gen. *Montgomery*.
James Weames, Gen. of the Ordinance.
Archibald Waddall, Adjutant Gen. of Foot
Marshall *White*.
Sam. Tavert, Quar. Ma. Gen. of the English Forces.
Alex. Harriot, Waggon Ma. Generall.
76 Cornets of Horse.
99 Ensignes of Foot.
90 Quarter Masters.
30 of the Kings Servants, whereof some are of quality.
9 Ministers.
9 Chirurgeons.
158 Colours.
The Kings Standard.
10,000 Prisoners.
Above 2,000, slaine.
All Armes, Bag and Baggage taken.
The Kings Coach and Horses, with much rich goods.
The Maior of *Worcester*.

from the impact of bullet, slash of sword or blow of a clubbed musket, but among them were nine captured Royalist surgeons, including Peter Barwick and James Davies (surgeon to the Lifeguards), all under the surgeon-general, Alexander Pennycuik of Edinburgh. These men treated the prisoners in their cramped and filthy prisons over the coming months. Surgeon Wiseman was captured after fleeing with the Horse and was imprisoned for many months at Chester. He later used his experiences as an army surgeon in the Civil War to write his major treatise in 1676 on the effect of musket wounds (*Of wound, of gun-shot wounds, of fractures and luxations*), using a number of examples from the battle of Worcester among his case studies.[3] The local civilian population would also have been expected to help care for the wounded, some of whom remained in Worcester for many months. But many of the most seriously wounded of the prisoners probably died in the days and weeks following the battle, either directly from their wounds or from shock or infection. Cromwell offered his own surgeon to treat the wounds of the Duke of Hamilton, who had been shot in the leg during the attack on Red Hill. He was taken back to his quarters in the Commandery, where, after the battle, the Royalist surgeon Kincaird and Cromwell's own surgeon Thomas Trappam (who had embalmed the body of Charles I) argued for five days over the merits and dangers of amputation. The delay in reaching a decision cost Hamilton his life and he died on 8 September, aged 35. His wife was refused permission to have his body brought home to Scotland and he was buried in Worcester Cathedral (where there is a small memorial). For the wounded on the Parliamentary side the situation was much better. The seriously wounded were carried to the Savoy and Ely House Hospitals in London; some were later brought to take the waters at Bath and some received pensions. One such was Christopher Ellin from the Essex militia, who had been shot in the arm and could no longer work as a blacksmith. By contrast, disabled Royalists had to wait until 1662 before they received any compensation.

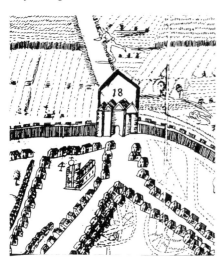

An integral part of the battle strategy had been to intercept any Scots that did try to make an escape from Worcester. The assumption was that they would try to retrace their line of march and Cromwell's carefully laid plan to position troops to block the likeliest escape routes proved extremely successful. The cavalrymen were pursued out of Worcester, through Barbourne and on the road north through

Detail of the plan of 1660, showing St Martin's Gate. (By courtesy of Worcester City Library)

120

The quayside. Many of the Scots surrendered here at the end of the battle, trapped against the quayside wall (left of picture). They were then herded into the Cathedral, in the background.

Kidderminster and into Shropshire, Cheshire and Lancashire by Harrison's cavalry brigade, which had reformed after its part in the assault of the city and now 'lapped them up as an ox lappeth up pastur'.[4] One column under Colonel Sanders was detached to pursue any that might try to flee through Derbyshire and Yorkshire. It would have been no mean feat to regroup the Horse with the sight of an open city, ripe for looting, before them! This must have been a terrifying experience for the hunted. In all, the Scots were pursued by around 4,000 Horse but they were also repeatedly ambushed by the troops that Cromwell had sited on their anticipated line of retreat and by the local population. Riding through the night some of the Scots were shot down when they were ambushed by the outlying garrisons at Bewdley and Kidderminster. Richard Baxter was woken up at Kidderminster by the sound of the fleeing horses on the cobbles. He described the scene when 'many hundreds of the flying army' were ambushed in the market-place by about thirty troopers sent the few miles from Bewdley. These may well have been part of the force dispatched to Bewdley just the day before the battle. 'And till midnight the bullets flying towards my door and windows, and the sorrowful fugitives hasting by for their lives, did tell me the calamitousness of war.'[5] Barton's Horse and Dragoons from Bewdley were alone reported as taking 1,200 prisoners.[6] Part of Cromwell's own regiment of Foot, detached before the battle, was part of the army intercepting the Scots in Shropshire and Cheshire. One of the officers, Captain John Hodgson, recorded in his diary how his men had 'pleasant work' with 500–600 of the exhausted Scots after blocking a road between Whitchurch and Nantwich. They were by now too weak to resist and Hodgson wrote: 'Our musketeers would have gone into the lane, and taken by the bridle the best-like person they saw, and brought him out, without a stroke, so low was the Scot brought.' The exhausted survivors of this engagement had no time to recover before falling into another ambush as they tried an alternative route towards Nantwich.[7] Here Colonel Lilburne's men blocked their further progress while 1,500 Horse and Dragoons who had pursued them from Worcester under Colonel Blundell attacked the column from the rear. In despair, many men now decided to give up and surrender. Another officer in Cromwell's regiment, Oliver Edge, was riding alone near Nantwich when he was confronted by a party of 18–20 horsemen who had escaped this ambush. After confirming that he was indeed an officer and therefore of an acceptable social status, the men insisted on surrendering to him. The surprised Edge had made a fine catch: his haul included the Earl of Derby, the Earl of Lauderdale and Lord Sinclair. These prisoners were taken first to Whitchurch in Shropshire, and then on to an inn at Bunbury in Cheshire on their way to Chester Castle. Arch-rivals Leslie and the wounded Middleton managed to flee as far as Rochdale before being captured; they were also imprisoned in Chester. Montgomery (also wounded), with eighty men, had tried to divert eastwards and flee into Yorkshire, but they were captured near Halifax. The chase was not without its cost to the Parliamentary forces. Northfield parish (now part of outer Birmingham) had to care for a number of wounded Parliamentary soldiers brought in up to 17 October.[8]

The pursuit of the fleeing Scots was not left up to the army alone, as local people, resentful of the new attempt to bring the country to Civil War, were eager to show their loyalty to the victorious Commonwealth and vent their feelings on the poor Scots. The Scots may or may not have plundered this area on their march in August 1651 but memories certainly extended back to the time when their predecessors had looted the locality in 1645. Cromwell reported that 'the country riseth upon them everywhere', and Clarendon later wrote 'very many of those who ran away were every day knocked in the head by the country people, and used with barbarity'.[9] This was one reason why it was eventually considered best to surrender to the army rather than risk trying to escape further. Tradition tells of villagers from Chaddesley Corbett in Worcestershire intercepting and killing stragglers at a road junction north of Barrett Hill, burying their victims in a simple roadside grave. Further afield, as around 1,000 of the Horse passed through Sandbach in Cheshire, they were set upon by local people armed with clubs, staves and even the poles taken from market stalls! The townsfolk retreated briefly when some of the Scots opened fire, but it appeared that only a few of the advance guard of fugitives actually had pistols and once they had passed through the people of Sandbach came out again and attacked the remainder with billhooks, capturing around 100 of them. It was a similar story at Congleton, where the countrymen would follow parties of Scots who would periodically turn and try to drive them off. The Congleton men shot a number of the Scots and took around 50 prisoners, including a Colonel Hamilton, and sent them to Chester.[10] It is not surprising, therefore, that Clarendon believed that these civilians acted far more cruelly than the soldiers in the heat of the battle. Those wounded Scots captured near Northfield perhaps fared better than most. One was tended for three weeks at a cost of 11s 2d before being carried away to prison (at a further cost of 1s).[11] A graphic description of the fears and emotions of the escaping Scots is contained in the account of one of their number riding with the main body of the escaping cavalry, who had managed to avoid the ambush at Nantwich and then the mêlée at Sandbach. He and his companions thought that they must by now have outridden their pursuers, but they had not counted on the careful preparations made before the battle for dealing with such a retreat or on the readiness of the local people to inform the military about the movements of the fugitives:

> our enemies' posts flew faster than we, and these wanted not considerable forces in every place to front us, and we were so closely pursued, in the day by the army and garrison forces, and in the night by the country, that from the time we came out of Worcester, until the Friday evening that I was taken prisoner seven miles from Preston, neither I nor my horse ever rested. Our body consisted of 3,000; in the day we often faced the enemy, and beat their little parties but still those of us whose horses tired or were shot were lost, unless they could run as fast as we rode. In the night we kept close together, yet some fell asleep on their horses, and if their horses tarried behind, we might hear by their cries what the bloody country people were doing with them.[12]

He was eventually captured near Preston.

Worcester Cathedral was used as a command post during the battle and as a prison to hold the Scots after the defeat of their army.

Lord Talbot managed to escape back to his family seat at nearby Longford House ($1^1/_2$ miles south-west of Newport) where he hid for a few days in an outhouse before being captured. Of the general officers, only the Duke of Buckingham escaped capture. His party escaped the ambush at Newport and reached Blore Park near Ashbourne, Staffordshire, on foot. There Buckingham exchanged clothes with a local labourer and was passed along a Royalist escape route to the house of Lady Villiers at Brooksby, Leicestershire. He eventually made his way to London where he reputedly disguised himself as an entertainer before escaping to the continent.

Cromwell wrote a triumphant letter to Parliament from Evesham on 5 September advising that he was about to deliver the prisoners into its hands. Somewhat taken aback by the unexpected speed of events, Parliament wrote to Cromwell on 6 September asking him not to be 'too speedy' in sending them to London. Meanwhile, the Council of State tried to work out what could be done with 10,000 new captives (following the similar number taken at Dunbar in the previous year). Open spaces and warehouses within the capital and hulks on the Thames were turned into temporary prison camps, with other prisoners dispersed to prisons around the country. At the same time the government tried to formulate a long-term strategy for dealing with them. In the context of the times Parliament believed that it was treating the prisoners leniently. True, there was an ominous request made to Cromwell by the Council of State in late September to 'prepare a narrative of the barbarous cruelties and murders committed by the Scottish people' upon their English prisoners, perhaps as a prelude to retaliation, but in pious tone Cromwell wrote on 2 October that he thought many of the Scots were godly but misguided, driven 'through weakness and the subtlety of Satan, involved in interests against the Lord and His people'. In the event few of the prisoners seem to have faced the death penalty, but their fate was not to be an easy one, despite Cromwell's assertion that they had been treated with 'tenderness'.[13]

The prisoners were first marched to their prisons, driven like cattle according to Clarendon. Those that arrived in London aroused considerable sympathy, with money and bread being thrown to them as they were marched by. Sir Richard Fanshawe, the King's Secretary, was in one convoy of hundreds of English and Scottish prisoners that was brought to London 'all naked on foot'. He had been reduced to accepting two women's shifts from Lady Denham at Bostal House in order to clothe himself.[14] In hiding at Mosely Hall near Wolverhampton on the evening of Tuesday 9 September, Charles II had witnessed a convoy of men described as Highlanders from his own regiment being marched to prison. They were

The cloisters of Worcester Cathedral would have been packed with exhausted and wounded Scots after the battle.

probably part of the Scottish Horse. Father Huddleston described them as 'all of them stript, many of them cutt, some without stockings or shoes and scarce so much left upon them as to cover their nakedness, eating peas and handfuls of straw in their hands which they had pulled upon the fields as they passed'. They were also forced to eat 'roots and raw coleworts cast out of gardens for hoggs'.[15]

Most of the prisoners were sent to London. By 9 September plans had been made to use as temporary prison camps the Tiltyard in Greenwich, the East India Company house and dockyard at Blackwall and the artillery ground in Tothill Field, Westminster. Chelsea College of Theology (later the Chelsea Hospital) and prison ships were also used. Other prisoners were scattered in miserable prisons across the country – at Shrewsbury, Stafford, Chester, Ludlow, Bristol and Worcester, and as far away as Newcastle and York. Some of the most fortunate of the prisoners were those taken to Nottingham. Here sympathetic local Presbyterians managed to have a number released and sent home with both new clothes and money.[16]

The greatest vengeance, in the first flush of victory when emotions were highest, was reserved for the English prisoners. The first to be captured in the campaign had been the 400 men of the Earl of Derby taken at Wigan in August. On 2 September orders were given to court-martial all the officers and every tenth common soldier; they would face execution, in the hope that this would dissuade any further Royalist support. The order was repeated after the battle of Worcester when at least five prisoners in Cheshire were executed. The Earl of Derby was beheaded in Bolton market-place on 15 October. His two lieutenants, John Benbow and Timothy Fetherstonhaugh, were also executed. Benbow was shot at Shrewsbury on 15 October and Fetherstonhaugh was beheaded at Chester on 22 October. It seems unlikely that all the sentences on the rest were actually carried out, as the usual practice in such instances would be for the condemned men to draw lots for who would actually be executed. Locally parish constables were ordered to give an account of any 'malignants' who had joined the Scottish army.[17] The English prisoners taken at Worcester were sent to London and held at St James's House and the Mews. On 16 October twenty of their number were also selected for court-martial but again there is no evidence that any death sentences were actually carried out (they were still alive on 6 November). Attitudes softened to some degree after it became clear that the threat of rebellion had been soundly beaten. In December it was eventually decided that the rest of the English prisoners were to be conscripted for military service in Ireland,[18] and thus many of the Royalists ended up fighting on behalf of the Commonwealth. It had been common practice throughout the Civil Wars for captured common soldiers to be offered their freedom in return for changing sides. A large part of the New Model Army after Naseby was actually composed of former Royalists.

The senior officers were imprisoned in Windsor Castle and the Tower of London. Some, such as Wemyss, Keith, Pitscottie and Leslie, languished there until the Restoration. While there, the melancholy Leslie turned to drink, facing repeated whispering as to his conduct during the battle. Efforts to make the Tower of London more comfortable from December 1651 led to a number of embarrassing escapes. Dalziel escaped from there in 1652 and took part in the Scottish rebellion of 1654. Massie recovered from his wounds and also eventually escaped from the Tower of London, spending the next few years in a succession of futile Royalist plots. Middleton also escaped from the Tower and returned to the King in exile, subsequently trying to organise further Scottish resistance in 1652. Another escapee was Colonel William Drummond, who entered the service of the Tsar before returning to the Restoration army in Scotland. The Mayor and Sheriff of Worcester were also temporarily imprisoned in the Tower but were released in January 1652. Presumably it was thought that they had been taught a sufficient lesson for surrendering the city.

A daily allowance of only $2\frac{1}{4}d$ for biscuit and cheese was provided to feed the common soldiers, with a higher rate for officers. None the less by 16 September it was costing £56 5s per day to feed them in London, suggesting that there were around 5,000–6,000 prisoners in the capital. Many died of starvation or disease. By 6 November there was such widespread infection among the English prisoners at St James's House that disease had also spread to the garrison set to guard them. A fever also spread through the prisoners held at Shrewsbury.[19] Holding the mass of prisoners in such conditions could only be a temporary expedient and more permanent options had to be sought to reduce their numbers as quickly as possible. On 25 September plans were laid to send individuals as servants to Members of Parliament and other loyal supporters. Cromwell had already made a present of two Scottish prisoners as servants to each of the members of the Parliamentary committee who came to greet him at Aylesbury after the battle. (The compassionate Whitelock had immediately sent his two prisoners back to Scotland!) Something on a wider scale was, however, required and in the next week a considerable number of officers below the rank of captain were exiled, many of them ending up as mercenaries on the continent, particularly in the army of the Russian Tsar. Some higher-ranking officers such as Lord Spynie, Lord Ogilvy, Lord Sinclair and the Earl of Crawford were also banished.[20]

The first solution arrived at in dealing with the bulk of the common

Scottish prisoners was to transport them to the New World colonies as indentured servants. This effectively made them slaves, albeit for a fixed period (usually seven years or more). This was by now a well-established practice for prisoners of war. In one order of 10 September 1,610 prisoners from Dunbar and probably also including men taken at Worcester were condemned to be transported to the tobacco plantations of Virginia. A formal committee to organise the transportation of prisoners from Worcester was appointed on 16 September. It was then agreed that a further 1,000 prisoners of the rank of lieutenant or cornet of Horse and below would be transported to the plantations of Virginia and New England. They were to be gathered from prisons in Chester, Shrewsbury, Stafford, Ludlow and Worcester, and taken to Bristol for transportation. The men were now regarded simply as a commodity, as part of a commercial contract organised with a number of traders. However, it was reported to the Council of State on 28 November that some of the merchants involved had broken their contract and some of these prisoners may not actually have been transported. As a consequence of the continued overcrowding disease had spread through the remaining prisoners in Bristol and by 2 December they had been dispersed to other prisons throughout the area.[21] On 21 October an order was given for the transportation of another consignment of prisoners to Bermuda.[22] At least one shipload of 1,500 men was also conveyed to the gold mines of Guinea.[23] The ill-fed prisoners were in a poor condition for such journeys, and merchants complained that many of the Scottish prisoners died before they could be shipped out.[24] Such comments were not made out of any sense of compassion but because they felt short-changed by the loss. As one small comfort for the transportees, Scottish ministers were to be transported free by the merchants – one per 200 men – and were to be allowed their freedom when they arrived. This was also a useful means of removing the Covenanter irritants within the Committee of Ministers. One group of 300 prisoners set sail on 8 November 1651 from London on the *John and Sara* under the command of Captain John Greene, bound for Charles Town, New England. They arrived there sometime before 24 February 1652.[25] They included men of the Grant, MacKannel, MacLean, Robinson, Ross, Simpson and Stewart clans. Twenty-eight of them died on board and the survivors were destined for the sawmills of Durham and Newmarket in New Hampshire, and the ironworks of Lynn. Although conditions were generally harsh, on occasion they received more compassionate treatment. In 1657 a 'Scottish Charitable Society' was founded in Boston 'for the relief of Scotchmen' after their term of transportation was completed.[26] Some men prospered: by 1665 the Scottish

minister of Ware parish in Virginia, Alexander Moray, who had himself
served in the army at Worcester, could write that many of the former
prisoners 'are now herein great masters of many servants themselves'.[27]
But few of these men ever returned home to Scotland.

There were great attractions for the government in passing the
responsibility for maintaining the prisoners into private hands. Other
approaches were therefore made from businesses closer to home. From
October a large number of the Scottish prisoners were transferred from
their prisons to a scheme to drain the fens of Norfolk and Cambridgeshire.
This was described by Samuel Pepys in 1663 as a 'heathened place', where
horses sank up to their bellies and where he was 'bit cruelly by gnats'.[28]
Malaria was endemic. The scheme was the construction of the New
Bedford River, designed by the Dutch engineer Cornelius Vermuyden on
behalf of the Company of Adventurers.[29] The artificial watercourse was
30 metres wide and 24 kilometres (15 miles) long, running south-to-north
from the River Ouse at Earith (Cambridgeshire) to the Denver Sluice
outside Downham Market (Norfolk). For a company that had met
widespread local opposition and was in financial difficulties, the supply of
cheap prison labour was a god-send. The Council of State authorised the
transfer of 1,000 men from Tothill Fields in London and also from York
prison to the scheme. On 14 October authority for the scheme was
extended to soldiers held at Newcastle and Durham. The prisoners were
warned that they would face the death penalty if they strayed more than
5 miles from their place of work. An escape rate of 10 per cent was
anticipated but the company would have to pay compensation of £5 per
man for any escapees above this level. The prisoners of war were to be
dressed in a prison uniform consisting of distinctive smocks made of white
kersey (a woollen cloth with a twill weave), with caps of a different colour.
This was so that they could be distinguished from the English workmen
and to make flight more difficult.[30] The headquarters of the operation was
probably in the 2-hectare Civil War fort at Earith between the Old and New
Bedford Rivers. One means that the Company of Adventurers found of
raising the revenue to pay for the prisoners' upkeep was to subcontract
them to local farmers to have their land 'hassacked' at the rate of 6s per
acre.[31] Problems continued over security and on 19 November Parliament
ordered that any Scot who tried to escape was to be put to death without
mercy. None the less the escapes continued, aided by the local inhabitants
who, aside from any sympathy that they might have felt for the prisoners,
also saw this as a means of disrupting the drainage scheme itself.[32]
Replacements were soon found and on 31 December the company agreed
to ship a further 500 prisoners from Durham to the port of King's Lynn for

the drainage works. By 9 January, in the midst of winter, many of the prisoners were described as being destitute, and 256 shirts, 128 suits (coat and breeches) and stockings were ordered for them. It would have been a miserable existence for the prisoners but by 1653 most of them had been allowed to return home, replaced by prisoners from the Dutch War. Some of the Scots did, however, settle permanently in the fenland.

With all other options of disposing of the prisoners in bulk explored, the only remaining practical course of action was simply to release the remainder. The only safeguard was to oblige them to sign an 'engagement' never again to take up arms against the Commonwealth. This had been a practice undertaken throughout the Civil Wars. On 17 December an order was granted allowing the very sick to be sent home, supplied with money and clothing, but also with a time limit by which time they had to complete their journey north of the border. The remaining English prisoners at St James's House and the Mews in London were also released at around the same time. Those prisoners still held at Newcastle, York, Durham, Shrewsbury and Gloucester were released throughout the first half of 1652, although some were still being held in Chester as late as August 1652.[33]

The minority of the Scottish soldiers who did eventually return to their homeland were penniless and proved to be a heavy burden on their already devastated communities – some turned to banditry and joined the bands of 'moss troopers'. The sequestration of estates had brought financial ruin to many of the Scottish gentry who had been involved. Many estates were left empty and the dispossessed therefore had little to lose in supporting the rising of 1654. In January 1656 Daniel Clerk, a former prisoner from the battle, had to petition to be given an allowance from his sequestered estate in Scotland in order to subsist and to pay off his debts.[34] Former English Royalists at the battle also took to highway robbery, including the most famous highwayman of his time, James Hind. He was reputed to have only robbed Parliamentarians! Hind was finally caught in 1652 and hanged in Oxford.

The human and economic cost of the battle was a national disaster for Scotland. Thousands of menfolk from the Camerons, MacGregors, Mackinnons, MacLeods, MacNabs and the other clans at the battle failed to return to their homes – they were either killed in battle, died in custody, were banished or were transported. The MacLeods lost between 50 and 80 per cent of their total strength of 1,000 men. Sir Robert of Opisdale (Clan Munro) had five sons at the battle, two of whom were killed; William was transported to Massachusetts, and Donald and Hector may have been transported to Barbados.[35] The fate of the men lost at Worcester could, for many, only be guessed. This could bring long-term complications for presumed widows who lacked clear proof that their husbands were now dead. Fifteen years after the battle, in 1666, a woman of the Clan Gunn had to search for witnesses to prove that her husband (a Robson) had been killed in the battle in order to be allowed to remarry. Despite such sacrifice, King Charles betrayed an ambivalent attitude towards his Scottish supporters, complaining that they had not fought effectively rather than praising them for having fought at all (unlike the majority of his supposed English supporters). It is not surprising that a number of the clans who had fought at Worcester bitterly refused to give any further support to the Stuarts.

Chapter Seven

The Escape of Charles II

there was no kind of misery (but death itself) of which His Majesty in this horrid persecution, did not in some measure, both in body, mind and estate, bear a very great share ...[1]

The dramatic escape of the King over a period of six weeks, with a £1,000 price on his head, has become an enduring romance of English history. The King himself frequently told the story, and his reminiscences were published from accounts told both on the voyage back to England in 1660 and twenty-nine years later in a dictation to Samuel Pepys.[2] Other accounts from those involved were published immediately after the Restoration in 1660 within Thomas Blount's *Boscobel*.[3] Even then, the legend was starting to overtake history.

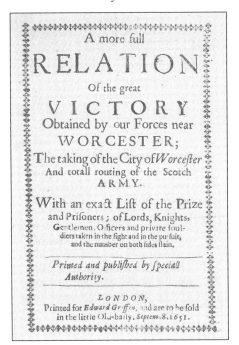

A more full

RELATION

Of the great

VICTORY

Obtained by our Forces near

WORCESTER;

The taking of the City of *Worcester* And totall routing of the Scotch ARMY.

With an exact List of the Prize and Prisoners; of Lords, Knights, Gentlemen, Officers and private souldiers taken in the fight and in the pursuit, and the number on both sides slain.

Printed and published by speciall Authority.

LONDON,
Printed for Edward Griffin, and are to be sold in the little Old-baily. Septem. 8. 1651.

The cover of a pamphlet advertising the victory at Worcester. (Reproduced with the permission of Worcestershire Record Office)

At first sight, with the country mobilised against him, the task seemed impossible. Charles had very distinctive looks: he was about 6ft 2in tall – a comparative giant of his time – with a swarthy complexion derived from the Italian blood in the French royal family. As a consequence the Parliamentary 'wanted' posters sought 'a tall black man, over two yards high'. He had a mass of black hair and heavy black eyebrows, with a curling mouth that was described as large and ugly. The one advantage that he had was that the search was for 'the King'. Apart from his followers at Worcester, if anyone had seen him in England it would have been as a teenager prior to his flight in 1646, with all the trappings of royalty about him – but he was to look very different during his escape in disguise as a gentlewoman's servant. He is a familiar image to us simply because the various portraits have become famous – but he would have been less familiar as a person to his subjects. None the less finding a disguise would have been difficult, even at the basic level of obtaining shoes to fit such a large man. More than this, however, Charles had to impersonate someone from a class that was foreign to him. He had to learn to walk without his regal gait, to be subservient and to handle the day-to-day tasks that would be expected of his guise – turning a spit or helping a lady mount a horse. Nevertheless, from the comfort of eventual success, this was a challenge that he seems to have relished as one of the great adventures of an eventful life. It is all the more remarkable given the failure of most of his companions to make good their escape.

Charles had left the remains of his army in Worcester at around 6pm. The initial escape was covered, albeit accidentally, by the crush of Scottish Horse around St Martin's Gate also trying to flee. Given the care that had been taken to block all other escape routes from the city, and the fact that the Scottish Horse had probably been carefully watched throughout the day by the Parliamentary cavalry, this at first sight seems strange. One might have expected the Parliamentary Horse to have charged the Scottish cavalry and St Martin's Gate in the final stages of the battle. Their failure to do so is probably a measure of the suddenness of events. Much of the Parliamentary Horse had been drawn off to join the storming of the city through Sidbury Gate. But once it became obvious that Leslie's cavalry was trying to escape then Whalley's Horse was ordered to make an immediate pursuit, quickly followed by a brigade under Harrison.

Charles and his immediate escape party, including the Duke of Buckingham, the Earl of Derby, the Earl of Lauderdale, Lord Wilmot, Colonel Blague and Lord Talbot, together with surviving members of the latter's troop of Horse, made a brief pause at Barbourne Bridge, 1,300m beyond the city defences, to decide which route to take. The Midlands Royalists would make a crucial contribution to the success of the mission. Charles was dissuaded from trying to reach London and instead decided to seek help from the Royalist Catholic underground movement in the Midlands. Their first guide would be local man Richard Walker, who had been a member of Lord Talbot's troop of Horse and a 'scout-master' (in charge of reconnaissance and spies). But their first problem was that they were still hemmed in by the remains of Leslie's Horse galloping past the King and his entourage in their attempt to escape back to Scotland. This made the body of men as a whole an obvious target. Twenty years later, remembering the failure of General Leslie to move out of Pitchcroft during the battle, Charles II's bitterness was still apparent when he complained: 'We had such a number of beaten men with us, of the horse, that I strove . . . to get from them; and though I could not get them to stand by me against the enemy, I could not get rid of them now I had a mind to it.'[4]

Following the line of march of the Scottish army in reverse, they rode through Ombersley to Hartlebury and then managed to separate from the main body of fugitives and turn east towards Stourbridge. 'We slipped away out of the high road that goes to Lancashire, and kept on the right hand, letting all the beaten men go along the front road.'[5] They therefore narrowly missed the first of the series of ambushes in Kidderminster.

THE KING'S ESCAPE

3 September	King flees Worcester at about 6pm.
4 September	Arrives at Whiteladies House, Boscobel, Shropshire. In evening stays with Francis Woolf at Madeley, Shropshire.
5 September	Day spent in Woolf's hayloft.
6 September	Returns to Boscobel House at about 3am. Hides for day in Boscobel Oak.
7 September	Goes to Madeley House, Staffs (now West Midlands).
8 September	Boscobel House searched by Parliamentarians.
9 September	Goes to Bentley Hall, Staffs (now West Midlands).
10 September	Begins escape with Jane Lane. Spends night at Long Marston, Warwickshire.
11 September	At Cirencester, Gloucestershire.
12 September	Arrives at Mr Norton's house, Abbots Leigh, near Bristol.
16 September	Leaves for Trent, Somerset.
22 September	Fails in attempt to find ship at Charmouth, Dorset.
6 October	At Heale House, Wiltshire.
12 October	Leaves for Hambleton, Wiltshire.
13 October	Arrives at George Inn, Brighton, Sussex.
15 October	Takes ship for France at 8am.
16 October	King lands in Normandy.

But the King was still accompanied by around 60 men. They rode through the night via Chaddesley Corbett and Hagley to Stourbridge and then into Shropshire. In a somewhat bizarre aristocratic concept of what constituted an unobtrusive disguise, the large party of armed gentry decided to speak French as they clattered through Stourbridge in the middle of the night. On the advice of the Earl of Derby, they were heading for the remote Boscobel House, then a hunting lodge deep within Brewood Forest. In the seventeenth century this was heavily wooded country and therefore ideal ground in which to hide a fugitive. Boscobel was owned by the Roman Catholic Giffard family and had been used as a temporary refuge by the Earl as he travelled south following his disastrous battle at Wigan. This would place the King in the hands of a well-organised Catholic underground movement based around a network of friends and servants of the Giffards. Fortunately, Charles Giffard was himself in the royal party. There was, however, a change of plan as to the final destination. Giffard may also have been concerned that Boscobel's earlier role as a Royalist hideout had already been discovered. Instead, they went to another of Giffard's properties, the isolated Whiteladies House, half a mile from Boscobel House and 26 miles from Worcester. They arrived here at about 3am on 4 September. Living there were Charles and George

Boscobel House, Shropshire, where Charles II hid after his escape.

Giffard and their wives, Mrs Anne Andrews, a priest (Father Walker), their woodman and servant John Penderel and his brother George. There were five Penderel brothers in all: William, the eldest, was a farmer and housekeeper at nearby Boscobel House, while Richard lived with their widowed mother at Hobbal Grange and Humphrey was a miller close to Whiteladies. They were Catholics, and George and John had served in the Royalist army during the First Civil War. Together they were to play a crucial role in the unfolding events.

Fortunately for Charles, most of his companions now decided to rejoin Leslie's cavalry, who were reported to be only a few miles away at Tong Castle. Many were captured shortly afterwards in an ambush at Newport, 6 miles away. The survivors were then involved in a running fight northwards to Nantwich where they were caught in yet another ambush. Charles Giffard was one of those said to have been captured there with the Earl of Derby. All of this would surely have driven home not only the scale of the Parliamentary forces now deployed against the fugitives but also how close they were to falling upon the King. A careless word at this stage could easily have betrayed him.

An immediate disguise for the King was needed: he had his hair cut short and was provided with less conspicuous countryman's clothing, consisting of a coarse hemp 'hoggen' shirt that quickly gave the King sores, a green doublet, grey breeches and a second, leather, doublet. The shoes were worn out and too small. They had to be slit to allow his feet to fit, giving him blisters. To complete the disguise, his face was dirtied with soot. He spent the next day in hiding in the nearby wood along with Richard Penderel. The pouring rain can only have darkened his mood still further. Large bodies of local militia under Colonel Ashenhurst were patrolling the roads from their headquarters at Cotsal, only 3 miles away, and capture must have seemed only a matter of time. Charles's first thought was to try to reach Wales with its strong tradition of Royalist support. He would go in disguise as a woodcutter called William Jones who was looking for work in the area. That evening Charles and Richard Penderel set off on foot to try to reach the house of yet another Roman Catholic, the 69-year-old Francis Woolf, at Madeley Hall, 9 miles away. The Hall was only $1\frac{1}{2}$ miles from a crossing over the River Severn but the area proved to be swarming with troops, and they had a scare 3 miles from their destination when they were heard by the miller from Evelith Mill, who chased them away. The final straw was the discovery that the river crossing was guarded by two companies of militia, and that all boats had been seized.

Charles concluded that any attempt to reach Wales was hopeless and, after hiding the next day in Woolf's hayloft, the disappointed fugitives

The royal oak, Boscobel.

turned back to Boscobel House. They arrived back there at about 3am. Here they met up with another of the officers from Lord Talbot's troop, a local man, Colonel Carlis. After a hurried breakfast of bread and cheese with a posset of thin milk and small beer, the two men were once again sent out into the woods to hide. It was here, on 6 September, that occurred perhaps the most famous episode of the whole escape. Charles and Carlis were forced to hide for the whole day, supplied with bread, cheese and small beer, in an oak tree in Boscobel Wood. The tree had been

The Penderel brothers escorted King Charles to Moseley Hall on the evening of 7 September (engraving from Thomas Blount's Boscobel *(1660)).*

well chosen. Although close enough to the house (137m) to allow a watch to be kept on it, the tree had been pollarded three or four years previously and the centre was therefore thick and bushy with new growth. Militia men searched close by, but did not pass the tree itself, and the King was at last able to get some sleep, resting on Carlis's cramped arm. There was now a reward of £1,000 posted for the King's capture and Charles momentarily doubted that anyone could resist such a bounty, but he was in safe and loyal hands with the five Penderel brothers. None the less William Penderel furthered the King's disguise by shaving him and again cutting his hair, this time 'as short at the top as the scissors would do it, but leaving some about the ears, according to the country mode'.[6] That night King Charles slept in a priest hole within the house. The small chamber, 1.2m x 1m and only 1.2m high, was built under the floorboards of the attic. John Penderel described him as being 'much dejected, having no hopes or prospect of redress'.

On the evening of Sunday 7 September the Penderels took the King to a reunion with Lord Wilmot, who had been moved on to Moseley Hall, near Wolverhampton, only 6 miles (9.6km) to the south-east of Boscobel. Like Boscobel it was a remote place, deep in the woods. The hall was owned by another Catholic, Thomas Whitgreave (1614–1702), who had served in the First Civil War under Thomas Giffard. Whitgreave was already sheltering a 23-year-old priest, Father Huddleston, who acted as a tutor to the children of the household. The five Penderel brothers, together with their brother-in-law Francis Yates, made an impressive, if conspicuous, escort as they brought Charles to Moseley. Each carried a pike or billhook and some had pistols. Two marched in front, one on each side and two behind. The King had an uncomfortable ride to within 2 miles of the house on a horse that he described as 'the heaviest dull jade he ever rode on'.[7]

The young Father Huddleston described his first sight of the King as the latter approached the back door of Moseley Hall. He wore

a very greasy old gray steeple-crowned hat, with the brims turned up, without lining or hatband, the sweat appearing two inches deep through it, round the band place; a green cloth jump coat, threadbare, even to the threads being worn white, and breeches of the same, with long knees down to the garter; with an old sweaty leathern doublet, a pair of white flannel stockings next to his legs, which the King said were his boot stockings, their tops being cut off to prevent their being discovered, and upon them a pair of old green yarn stockings, all worn and darned at the knees, with their feet cut off . . . his shoes were old, all slashed for the ease of his feet, and full of gravel, with little rolls of paper between his toes . . . he had an old coarse shirt, patched both at the neck and the hands, of that very coarse sort which, in that country, go by the name of hogging shirts . . .[8]

The shoes and stockings were apparently not even matching pairs. The tops of the boot stockings had been cut off because they were embroidered and were therefore too obviously rich for the rest of the ensemble. Lord Wilmot must have been appalled by the spectacle. He was the quintessential cavalier, aged 38 and full of bravado to the point of indiscretion. Throughout the adventures of the royal escape he refused to be parted from his horse and his only concession to a disguise was to carry a hawk on his arm and pretend to be a gentleman out hunting![9] Nevertheless the strategy was so bold and simple that it worked and Wilmot made good his escape with the King. Wilmot had made contact with the 42-year-old Colonel John Lane of nearby Bentley Hall, 5 miles (8km) to the south-east. Lane's younger brother Richard had been in the Royalist army at Worcester and no doubt the Colonel was eager for news. (In fact Richard was safe among the prisoners.) This meeting led to an important piece of luck. At a time when it was impossible to move freely around the country, the Colonel's sister Jane had obtained a pass from the governor of Stafford to take herself and a manservant to Bristol in order to be with a friend, Ellen Norton, who was expecting a child. The new plan was for King Charles to impersonate this servant and to try to find a ship for the continent at Bristol or on the south coast. Wilmot would travel independently in order to arrange contacts with local Royalists. Colonel Carlis now also agreed to separate and make his own escape.

Parliamentary troops were now closing in on the Catholic underground and the King. A prisoner taken in Cheshire had told his captors that the royal party had ridden to Whiteladies House and this was consequently searched from top to bottom. In answer to some rough questioning, George Giffard claimed that a party of Royalists had certainly ridden through, but he had not known if the King was among them. An attempt was even made to search Moseley while the King was hidden in a priest hole (traditionally that on the first floor, below a wardrobe), but this was cunningly foiled by Whitgreave who made a great show of leaving doors open to prove that he had nothing to hide.[10] The King remained there in hiding until Tuesday night. At midnight on 9 September Colonel Lane collected Charles to take him to Bentley Hall and the next morning Charles began his hazardous journey to the south coast with Jane Lane. They were accompanied by her cousin Henry Lascelles, who had served as a cornet to Colonel Lane in the First Civil War. The King's role was as the son of one of Jane Lane's tenant farmers, acting as her attendant for the journey. He was disguised in the grey Sunday-best suit of a poor farmer, and went by the name of Will Jackson. The King described the next stage of the journey:

> We took our journey towards Bristol, resolving to lie at a place called Long Marson [Long Marston], in the Vale of Evesham. We had not gone two hours on our way before the mare I rode cast a shoe, so we were forced to ride to get another shoe at a scattering village, whose name began with something like 'Long –', and as I was holding my horse's foot I asked the smith the news. He told me there was no news that he knew of, since the good news of the beating of the rogues, the Scots. I asked him whether there were none of the English taken that joined with the Scots. He answered that he did not hear that rogue, Charles Stuart, was taken, but some of the others, he said, were taken, but not Charles Stuart. I told him if that rogue were taken he deserved to be hanged more than all the rest for bringing in the Scots, upon which he said I spoke like an honest man, and so we parted.

This oft-recalled incident may have been at Longborough.[11] Later stories also claim that they spent a day on this journey in the woods behind Bously Lodge in Alvechurch parish (on the route from Bentley Hall to Long Marston).[12] From there they went to Stratford where they had to manoeuvre past a troop of Parliamentary Horse and then spend a night with friends of Jane Lane (John and Amy Tomb) at Long Marston. There the King had to act out his role of a clumsy gentleman servant in the kitchen, failing to work the spit properly. They spent the night of Thursday 11 September at the Crown Inn, Cirencester. The King and Henry Lascelles shared a room but, as befitted his role as servant, 'Will Jackson' was only given a truckle-bed, pulled out from beneath the four-poster bed. When left alone, Henry generously swapped beds with his sovereign.

From Cirencester the party passed through Bristol and arrived at their official destination, the Norton household at Abbots Leigh (a few miles to the west of Bristol and overlooking the Bristol Channel) on the Friday. Here occurred another famous encounter as the King met a man who claimed (possibly untruthfully) to be a soldier from the King's Lifeguard, but failed to recognise his sovereign and indeed said that the King was at least three fingers taller. The butler at the house, John Pope (a former servant at Court who had served in Colonel Bagot's regiment at Lichfield during the First Civil War), did, however, recognise him but remained loyal and was sent out to discover details of any suitable shipping leaving Bristol. Unfortunately there was none available and so, after a brief rendezvous with Lord Wilmot, who had also made his way south, the King set off on

Tuesday 16 September towards the south coast. They were now heading for Trent Manor (approximately 40 miles south of Abbots Leigh on the Somerset/Dorset border near Sherborne), the home of Colonel Wyndham, who had been the Governor of Dunster Castle during the First Civil War. Fearing that the coast would be heavily guarded, it was hoped that this would serve as a more inconspicuous base while looking for a ship. Jane Lane and Henry Lascelles at this point headed back home before making their own escape to France, fearing that their part in the escape would soon become known.

While at Trent Manor Charles was obliged to listen to the sounds of celebration from the nearby village as the occupants entertained a trooper who claimed to have personally killed the King at the battle of Worcester. Along with much drinking, the church bells were rung, guns fired and bonfires lit. According to the then 19-year-old Lady Anne Wyndham, writing in 1681, such popular expressions of disloyalty did not engender any outward sign of anger or bitterness within the King but merely pity – 'Alas, poor people!', he cried.[13] His more private thoughts were not recorded, although he cannot but have contrasted such a joyous reaction to his defeat with the confident promises of countrywide support that his courtiers had regaled him with while in exile. Unfortunately for Charles there was a great shortage of vessels in the area as many had been pressed into service to carry the army to Jersey (which still held out for the King). This also meant that there were large bodies of troops in the area. Fortunately the government seemed to have little idea of where the King might actually be. Rumours abounded. Reports were published that the King was on his way to Scotland or the Isle of Man, or even that he had joined a highwayman near Coventry.[14]

The first attempt was made to board a coal ship at Charmouth, Dorset, just north of Lyme Regis. The owner, Captain Ellesdon, who was known to have helped previous fugitives, was simply told that some escapees from the battle of Worcester needed passage to France. Proceedings then turned to farce as the wife of the ship's captain, Stephen Limbrey, discovered what was afoot and locked her husband in the bedroom to prevent him from getting involved in such a dangerous venture![15] The escape party had taken a room in the Queen's Arms at Charmouth and the suspicions of the ostler, Henry Hall, who was a member of the local militia, had been aroused by the comings and goings of his guests as they waited for the arrival of the King. In particular he noticed that they kept their horses saddled all night ready for a rapid departure. Hall was not satisfied by the cover story that was circulated to the effect that the conspirators were simply planning an elopement between two ill-starred lovers (acted out by the King and the niece of Lady Anne Wyndham, Juliana Coningsby). His suspicions that these were actually senior Royalists planning an escape seemed to be confirmed when he was told by the local smith that Lord Wilmot's horse had been shod in three different counties, including Worcestershire. It is not clear how he reached that conclusion and it is possible that it was a later embroidery of the story. But the ostler did pass on his suspicions to the local parson, Benjamin Westley, who guessed that this might be the royal escape party. Hall then decided to inform his commanding officer in the militia. The local military were mobilised and searched the inns and the houses of several known Royalists in the area, convinced that the King was trying to escape dressed as a woman. But the royal party had already fled Charmouth, fearful of the non-appearance of Limbrey's ship. They had first gone to Bridport and then on to Broadwindsor in Dorset. All the time they had to pass through troops mobilising for the invasion of Jersey, and with a party of a dozen troopers now in pursuit. They took shelter in rooms on the top floor of the George Inn in Broadwindsor, but then the rest of the inn was commandeered by around 40 soldiers who were passing through to the coast ready for embarkation. The king was trapped and might have expected to be discovered at any moment. The soldiers were, however, accompanied by some of their families and camp followers, including a pregnant woman who promptly went into labour. The noise of her labour pains was accompanied by fierce arguments between the soldiers and the officers of the parish as to who would be responsible for maintaining the mother and child when the soldiers moved on. This was all sufficient distraction to ensure that Charles spent the night if not in peace then at least in relative safety.[16] Meanwhile, an embarrassed Ellesdon had gone to the house of Sir Hugh Wyndham (uncle of Francis Wyndham) at Pilisdon House, Devon, looking for the King. It appears that he had been followed by soldiers from Charmouth as the house was raided soon afterwards. The troopers treated the household roughly and 'did not spare the young ladies'.[17]

Disappointed at this failure to find a ship, the King returned inland to Trent Manor. The area was clearly becoming dangerous and he had been a fugitive at Trent for nineteen days – too long for safety. On 3 or 6 October (accounts vary) he was therefore moved by 'private ways' further inland to Heale House on the River Avon near Salisbury, home of the widow Katherine Hyde (a cousin of Clarendon). He stayed there for four or five nights while Wilmot sought contacts with local known Royalists. It was difficult for an over-awed Katherine to maintain the alias of the King in front of her servants. One night at supper he was seated at the lower end of the dining table as befitted his assumed lowly position, but she could not resist giving him two larks to eat when everyone else was only given one![18] Meanwhile Wilmot's continuing enquiries had led him to Colonel George Gunter from Racton, near Chichester, and together they scoured the Sussex coast for a ship. Eventually Gunter decided to risk approaching an acquaintance, the Chichester merchant Francis Mansell, who regularly traded with France and might therefore have some useful shipping contacts. Gunter claimed to want passage for two friends who had been involved in a duel. Mansell agreed to help and went with Gunter to Brighton where they eventually made contact with Nicholas Tettersell, the master of the 34-ton coal-ship *Surprise*. After a long negotiation, Tettersell agreed to carry the 'duellists'.

The King left Heale House at 2am on Sunday 12 October and started his ride eastwards towards the Sussex coast, resting overnight at the house of Gunter's brother-in-law Thomas Symons at Hambledon. Thomas Symons came in drunk and in some confusion at first mistook the King, with his short haircut and in the dress of a 'meaner sort of country gentleman', for a Roundhead colonel![19] Thomas was rewarded at the Restoration with the appropriate gift of a drinking cup. They finally reached Brighton where the party, now consisting only of the King, Wilmot and Gunter, took a room at the George Inn on West Street (later renamed the King's Head.) A last-minute crisis arose when Tettersell realised who his passengers were and demanded a higher fee for the risk involved. King Charles smoothed the situation and around 4am on Wednesday 15 October he and Wilmot finally boarded the ship at anchor in Shoreham Creek. They set sail at about 8am and were put ashore at dawn the next morning at Fécamp harbour in Normandy. When Charles arrived in Paris the Venetian ambassador reported how 'his dress was more calculated to move laughter than respect, and his aspect is so changed that those who were nearest believed him to be one of the lower servants'.[20] One may wonder which reaction Charles hated worst – the ridicule or the pity. Charles was to spend the next nine years in exile.

In 1681 Thomas Blount described the emotion of the flight.

From the 3 of September at Worcester to the 15 of October at Brighthemston being one and forty dayes. He passed through more dangers than he travailed miles, of which yet he travers'd in that time only neer three hundred (not to speak of his dangers at Sea, both at his comming into Scotland, and his going out of England nor of his long march from Scotland to Worcester) some-times on foot with uneasy shooes; at other times on horseback, encumbered with a portmanteau and which was worse, at another time, on the gall-back'd slow paced

Millers horse; sometimes acting one disguise in course linnen and a leather doublet; sometimes another, of almost as bad a complection; one day he is forced to sculke in a barn at Madely; another day sits with Colonel Carlos [sic] in a tree, with his feet extremely surbated and at night glad to lodge with William Penderel in a secret place at Boscobel which never was intended for the dormitory of a King.

Sometimes he was forced to shift with coarse fare for a belly-full; another time in a wood, glad to relieve the necessities of nature with a messe of milk served up in an homely dish by good-wife Yates a poor country woman. Then again for a variety of tribulation, when he thought himself almost out of danger, he directly meets some of those rebels, who so greedily sought his bloud, yet by God's great providence, had not the power to discover him; and (which is more than has yet been mentioned) he sent at another time to some subjects for relief and assistance in his great necessity who out of a pusillanimous fear of the bloudy Arch-rebel then reigning, durst not own Him.

Besides all this twas not the least of his afflictions daily to hear the Earl of Derby and other his most loyal subjects, some murdered some imprisoned and others sequestred in heaps, by the same bloudy usurper, only for performing their duty to their lawful King. In a word there was no kind of misery (but death itself) of which His Majesty in this horrid persecution, did not in some measure, both in body, mind and estate, bear a very great share . . .

Later in Paris (and much against the advice of his wife), Charles bitterly complained in public against the Scots 'for using him serviley, heaping indignities upon him'. Despite the fact that his English followers had provided virtually no support at Worcester, contrary to the promises made while he was in exile, he felt particularly let down by the Scottish troops at Worcester.[21] Significantly, soon after the Restoration (22 May 1661) the Covenant that he had been obliged to sign was ordered to be burnt by the common hangman throughout London.

Charles remained in exile until May 1660. Ironically his Restoration was achieved in large part through the support of the same New Model Army that had destroyed his effort to win back his throne by military might in 1651. His procession into London was lined by cheering crowds – the same people who had flocked to join Fleetwood's and Skippon's militias and who had taken part in the battle of Worcester.

Chapter Eight

A Tour Around the Battlefield

Much of the Worcester battlefield is now built over by modern development, still bisected by the River Severn. The new southern ring-road further interrupts the sense of battlefield landscape. Only a small part (beside the Teme) has been formally classed as a 'battlefield' on the Register maintained by English Heritage. None the less it is still possible to get a sense of the flow of the battle and the way that the contemporary landscape affected events. The tour of the battlefield naturally falls into three parts, reflecting the main stages of the battle from the initial crucial crossing of the Severn at Upton-upon-Severn (Tour 1), to the attack across the River Teme (Tour 2) and the final stage of the fighting within Worcester itself (Tour 3).

Tour 1 – Upton-upon-Severn

In Upton-upon-Severn park in the public car park (SO 8501 4077) on the north edge of the town on the main road to Worcester (B4211). Walk right into the town, past the church tower, and turn left down High Street to the riverside. This was the site of the bridge in the seventeenth century with access on the east bank along what is now East Waterside. The bridge collapsed in 1852 and was rebuilt (the bridge abutments still survive). The present bridge was constructed 82m to the north in 1940. On the morning of 28 August 1651 a small party of dragoons from General Lambert's force, sent the previous day from Evesham, crossed the part-demolished bridge from the east bank into Upton. Initially they took the small garrison of Scots by surprise but once spotted they were forced to take shelter in the nearby church. Walk back up High Street and turn right into Church Street. On the right is the surviving fourteenth-century tower of the church, with its distinctive cupola of 1769–70. The rest of the church was demolished in 1937 and the building is now a heritage centre, including a small display on the Civil War. The eighteen Parliamentary dragoons were besieged in the church by the enraged Scots, but while the attentions of the latter were diverted, more Parliamentary troops forded the river 150m to the south beside Fisher's Row and charged the Scots. If you turn to face the south and the heavily restored early seventeenth-century Anchor Inn you can imagine Parliamentary Horse and Dragoons pouring out of Dunn's Lane and London Lane. They chased the Scots back along Church Street and the main road towards Worcester. Follow the line of the retreat past the car park and the brick-built Severn Cottage. It was here that the Scots made their last stand behind a slight earthwork thrown up to block the road to Worcester. Other Parliamentary troops had swept through Upton and also charged this position from Hyde Lane. The now-outflanked Scots then finally retreated back to Worcester. By the next day 12,000 Parliamentary troops had been brought from Evesham to Upton. Cromwell visited his men on 29 August and was greeted 'with abundance of joy and extraordinary shouting from his elated troops' before returning to the rest of his army, then marching from Evesham to Worcester. The capture of the river crossing was of vital importance to Cromwell's final success. After being rested, the troops then formed the main assault force of the Parliamentary army on 3 September, marching the 9 miles to Worcester and forcing the crossings over the River Teme.

If you journey by car up the B4211/B4424 you will reach Powick and the starting point of Tour 2 at Powick Church.

Tour 2 – Powick to Teme

This tour follows the line of advance of the Parliamentary army from Powick church to Powick Bridge and the Teme crossing over the bridge of boats. From the conclusion of Tour 1 at Upton-upon-Severn follow the B4211 and its change into the B4424 into Powick and park at Powick church, on the right (SO 8343 5153). If approaching from the A422 southern ring-road around Worcester, take the A449 to Malvern and after about 700 yards (640m) take the B4424 to Upton-on-Severn. Almost immediately on the left is the driveway to Powick church. The church stands on the east end of a low ridge and was a forward observation post for the Scots prior to the battle. Parliamentary troops also camped around here prior to the skirmish at Powick Bridge in September 1642. Walk around to the south side of the church. The walls of the tower have the marks of a round of case-shot from light artillery or musket fire on the bottom storey and up towards the parapet. Although such marks are not unknown from places without Civil War connections (the nineteenth-century Rifle Volunteers were well known to take the occasional pot-shot at church towers!), in this instance their context is most likely the initial stage of the battle of 3 September 1651. The Parliamentary army was approaching from the south from Upton-on-Severn and an observation post on top of the tower was probably dislodged by fire from the Parliamentary advance guard. Fleetwood's army could then occupy the ridge of high ground and make ready to sweep down on to the floodplain and the crossing-point of Powick Bridge. The church tower would now make an ideal observation platform for Fleetwood, with good views across the whole west battlefield.

Walk back to the main road and turn right (north) towards Worcester. In 1651 Powick was just a small hamlet, surrounded by a network of hedged fields and narrow lanes. The field patterns that are visible below the church still give a flavour of the seventeenth-century landscape, although the actual ground level on the floodplain has risen considerably over the past 350 years owing to repeated flooding. There was a running fight from the church to Powick Bridge. Musket-balls have been found behind the Red Lion public house and to the left was 'Slaughter Furlong'. Cross the modern A422 ring-road and walk down the original road leading to the medieval Powick Bridge, to the west of the modern road bridge (SO 8352 5250). This narrow lane, bounded by tall hedges, will again give the feel of the battlefield landscape in this area. The bridge was built in the fifteenth century and proved to be a major obstacle during the battle. It was only wide enough for four men to march abreast and the two inner spans of the bridge had been demolished prior to the battle. The extent of the subsequent repair is visible in the different stonework. The main Scottish

Beside Powick Bridge is the modern memorial to the Scottish casualties from the battle. The emphasis on the unity of the Scottish army is a product of modern romanticism!

position under Keith's Highlanders guarding the bridge was in the mill building, now built over by the converted power station.

Apart from its role in the battle of Worcester, Powick Bridge was also the focus of what was regarded by contemporaries as the first skirmish of the Civil Wars on 23 September 1642. A Parliamentary force of 500–1,000 Horse and Dragoons under Colonel John Brown were shadowing a treasure convoy that had camped on the city side of Powick Bridge. The Parliamentarians had taken up a position around Powick church. Hearing a rumour that the Royalists, under Sir John Byron, were preparing to make a dash for Shrewsbury, Brown brought his men down from Powick. While his main force formed up on Powick Ham, an advance guard under Colonel Edwin Sandys charged the bridge. The small force of only 200 Royalists had, however, been reinforced by another 500 Horse under Prince Rupert, who were camped in the field just beyond the bridge. Both sides seemed equally surprised by this turn of events but the Royalists recovered first and drove Sandys's men off the bridge. Some were pushed over the bridge and drowned, others were trampled in the narrow lane leading to the bridge. Panic ensued in the Parliamentary ranks and they retreated back to Pershore. Although the total casualties were small (with the dead being buried in St John's churchyard), the psychological impact was enormous, not least for establishing the reputation of Prince Rupert as a dashing and skilful cavalry commander. More than any other location, therefore, Powick Bridge has justifiable claims to be the place 'where England's sorrows began, and where they are now happily ended'.

Walk east along the footpath running a mile along the north bank of the Teme to its confluence with the Severn. In doing so, you will pass a memorial beside the bridge, erected to commemorate the Scottish dead of the battle. This is where the small Scottish force managed to hold off Fleetwood's army for over an hour, lining the riverbank and the hedge lines behind it. The bridge of boats across the Teme was just above its confluence with the River Severn. Near its site, on the south bank of the river, are two hollows that may mark the site of burial pits from the battle. These were noted in the nineteenth century and there are records of human bones being discovered during ploughing. It was the responsibility of local people to bury the dead from a battle and in this part of the battlefield this duty may have fallen on the inhabitants of Powick parish, who brought the dead on the north side of the river back to the margin of their own parish for burial.

Walk around to the Severn. A second bridge of boats was constructed here, some 45m above the confluence with the Teme. Cromwell led his New Model Army cavalry down a natural ravine approximately 200m from the confluence, where the slope was shallower, before crossing the bridge and breaking the stalemate of the battle. They drove the Scottish defenders away from the bridgehead, giving Fleetwood the opportunity to start to move his men across. They then fanned out across the fields, fighting from hedgerow to hedgerow. Walk back towards Powick Bridge, following the line of the expanding bridgehead. The defenders of Powick Bridge realised that they were in danger of being outflanked, especially as Colonel Haines had managed to get part of his regiment to wade across the Teme about a mile north of the bridge. The Scots therefore withdrew from their positions around Powick Mill back along the lane leading towards St John's. This gave the opportunity for planks to be thrown across the part-demolished bridge, enabling more of Fleetwood's troops to make the crossing. The Parliamentary army was now advancing along a 2-mile (3.2km) front into St John's with their goal being the bridge across the Severn into Worcester itself.

From the riverbank there is a clear view of Worcester Cathedral. The reverse view of this part of the battlefield from the Cathedral was, however, obscured by the hedges running across the flat landscape and on the day itself by the smoke rising from the battlefield. Walk up the Malvern Road (A449) into Worcester to Manor Farm (farm shop and public house on the right). This road was described as being lined with the Scottish dead during the Parliamentary advance. From the grounds of the farm shop (which contains a small display of artefacts recovered from the battlefield) you can look back towards the Teme for a Royalist view of the battle landscape.

Tour 3 – Worcester

The best place to get an overall impression of the battlefield of 3 September is from the top of the Cathedral tower in Worcester city centre. Binoculars are advised. (Visitors should check with the Cathedral authorities in advance for opening times to the tower.) The Cathedral became directly involved at a number of stages during the Civil Wars. It was used as an arms store by the Royalists in September 1642 and was then ransacked by the army of the Earl of Essex. Light cannon were even mounted on the tower during the siege of 1646. The fabric was allowed to decay during the Civil War, with the 64m-high detached bell tower on the north side (then being used as a wood shed) being sold in 1647 for its lead roof and other building materials for £617 4s 2d. The money was supposed to go towards the repair of the almshouse and a number of churches, but some was still in hand in 1651 and was used to compensate Parliamentary supporters whose property had been looted by the Scots.

Charles II held a council of war with his generals on top of the tower before, and in the opening stages of, the battle of Worcester. They would have struggled, as we do today, with the narrow spiral staircase in the upper stages of the fourteenth-century tower. Immediately after the battle the Cathedral was used as the prison for the bulk of the 10,000 Scottish prisoners captured in the city. The conditions would have been appalling, at least as bad as in the Guildhall which had to be disinfected afterwards. Once you have climbed the 52m-high tower you will be rewarded with a panoramic display of Worcester and the surrounding landscape, still giving a feel of what Charles II would have seen on the morning of 3 September.

Looking to the south, you can follow the line of the River Severn downstream to the Teme junction (note that in the seventeenth century the 'island' at Diglis locks did not exist). In the distance (on a clear day and with binoculars) can be seen the high ground on the east bank where Cromwell led the charge across the bridge of boats. To the right, just over 1½ miles (2.5km) away, you may be able to identify the former power station chimney which is immediately adjacent to Powick Bridge. To the left of the chimney and further in the distance is the squat tower of Powick Church (over 2 miles/3.4km). You will, however, easily appreciate the difficulty of picking out details at this distance. The line of the Teme and its junction with the Severn are lost in the pattern of hedgerows – probably much as they were in 1651, the more so if the air was filled with the billowing clouds of musket smoke. Charles was therefore obliged to ride down to the Teme to assess for himself the situation on the ground. This is the area you can visit as part of Tour 2. Although details may have changed, the pattern of hedgerows visible beside the river and down towards Powick is probably much as it was in the seventeenth century. This proved to be a major handicap in the Parliamentary advance. In the foreground is the site of the castle, a ruin even in the seventeenth century and now completely levelled and built over. In the middle of the battle Cromwell ordered part of the army on the west bank of the Severn to cross back and attack the city through what is now Diglis and storm the defences below the castle on Severn Street.

Looking to the east, the situation of Worcester overlooked by the rim of high ground on the east side is very clear. The line of the city defences runs along the nearside of the City Walls Road (behind the cinema complex) and then through the King's Head public house to the London Road. Just to the north of this is the Commandery, the headquarters of the Duke of Hamilton during the Scottish occupation. In the middle distance is Fort Royal, now an urban park. The fort was probably built during the First

Civil War but greatly enlarged by the Scots in 1651. The triangular south-west bastion is clear. The ditch in front of the fort has now been backfilled and the whole feature softened by landscaping. The fort overlooked the original line of London Road. In the seventeenth century the road ran further to the south than the present route, which was cut into the south side of Fort Royal in the eighteenth century. The original line of London Road bent more around the natural gradient of the hill. The fort protected the city from the higher ground to the east. Here lies Red Hill, with Perry Wood to the north. The line of hills was occupied by Parliament on 30 August. The area of modern housing to the left of Fort Royal was open ground in the seventeenth century, and was partly a poorly drained bog. At 4pm Charles mounted his counter-attack using Fort Royal as forward support. Charles led one arm of a pincer movement up London Road to attack Red Hill from the south. Middleton and Hamilton led the north arm of the attack up a ravine on the north side of Perry Wood. But the attack failed, Fort Royal was captured and the Scots tried to escape back into the city through Sidbury Gate, hotly pursued by Parliamentary cavalry and militia.

Looking to the north, the seizure of control over the west bank of the Severn bounding Worcester was probably the primary objective of the initial Parliamentary battle plan for 3 September. In the seventeenth century the Severn Bridge stood between the modern bridge and the railway viaduct. On the east side of the river, beyond the bridge and the line of the defences (running inside the line of the later railway viaduct), is the open space of Pitchcroft, now the racecourse (1,000yd/900m from the Cathedral). This was the traditional site of the musters of the Worcestershire Trained Bands during the seventeenth century and during the Scottish occupation was the camp of the Scottish Horse. On the west bank of the river is the approach road to the then small hamlet of St John's. The river crossing on this side was protected by a large triangular bastion. The proximity of Pitchcroft to the crossing over the Severn is clear, yet only limited reinforcements were sent from the city to the hard-pressed troops trying to stem the tide of Fleetwood's advance through St John's. For whatever reason, the troops in the city looked on as their comrades on the west side of the river were finally forced to surrender. Later in the battle General Leslie also refused to provide support from Pitchcroft to the troops battling on Red Hill. He may have been focusing instead on finding an escape route back to Scotland with his men. Closer to the Cathedral, the open car park adjacent to the east bank of the Severn (on Copenhagen Street) marks the location of the final surrender of the bulk of the Scottish troops, pushed back against the quay wall and the riverside. The majority

The Cathedral Green, looking towards the site of St Michael's Church. Many of the Scottish dead were buried here. Appropriately, this is now the site of the civic war memorial.

of the prisoners were then herded into the Cathedral. Others were imprisoned in the Guildhall.

Now descend the tower. When you leave the Cathedral from the main entrance, outside and to the right is the site of St Michael Bedwardine. The parishioners were forced to bury many of the dead from the battle in their churchyard. Coincidentally this is now the site of the civic war memorial. Walk down Sidbury towards the gate (marked by a plaque on the side of the King's Head public house, no. 67) and the Commandery museum. You are following the route of one of the final desperate charges of the Royalist Horse in the city, hoping to stem the Parliamentary advance. The Commandery was Hamilton's headquarters and is now a museum with displays on the Civil War. (The name itself has nothing to do with the Civil War but refers to the building's former history as a medieval hospital with connections to the Knights Hospitaller.) After the battle the Commandery was used as a hospital for wounded prisoners, including Hamilton himself. The room where the latter is traditionally thought to have died is still known as the 'Hamilton Room'. Willis Bund, writing in 1913, reported that until recently a dark stain on the floor of that room was said to have been Hamilton's blood! This room was part of the family quarters of the seventeenth-century house and would have provided some degree of comfort. The rest of the wounded were probably contained in the open hall, service ranges and even outside in the garden. Here there is also a small memorial to the dead of both sides during the Civil Wars. Details of opening hours can be obtained from the Tourist Information Office or from the website at http://www.worcestercitymuseums.org.uk.

Passing the Commandery, turn left on to Wyld's Lane and then climb the hill to the right on to Fort Royal. The best view is from the surviving triangular artillery bastion (now a flower-bed) on the south side, adjacent to the London Road. Originally it was surrounded by a wide ditch with an earthen rampart, linked by a covered way leading back to the Commandery. The bastions carried the Scottish leather cannon that were intended to defend the city from the Parliamentary positions on the higher ground to the east and to protect the entry along the London Road. Looking east one can see the ring of high ground of Red Hill and Perry Wood. At about 5pm the Essex militia swept down from the high ground, stormed the ditch and rampart and massacred the defenders of Fort Royal. This was the moment at which Cromwell decided to change the plan of battle and launch an all-out attack on the city. You are standing at the point of some of the most bitter fighting of the battle. Turning towards the city it is clear how, once captured, the fort and its cannon would dominate the city. Parliamentary Horse, followed by the Cheshire militia, charged down the London Road through Sidbury Gate, while the Essex militia mopped up resistance to the north of the fort.

You can now follow the progress of the Parliamentary army as they stormed the town. Retrace your steps back down Sidbury, pausing at the site of the gate. Imagine hundreds of fleeing Scottish soldiers trying to escape back into the city, with Whalley's troopers at their backs. The temporary barricade of an overturned cart was pushed aside and then the Parliamentary army stormed the city. If you turn right along City Walls Road you will see surviving stretches of the medieval city wall, partially razed after the battle of Worcester. The medieval ditch ran approximately along the line of the present road. But in this part of the city it is likely that the ground, with a network of drainage ditches, was left as a bog during the Third Civil War. The spur of defences built during the Civil War joined the medieval defences around 'blockhouse fields' (now just past the rear of the cinema complex). Turn left into the Cornmarket. This is close to the site of St Martin's Gate, from where Charles II made his escape from the city at about 6pm. On the corner of Cornmarket and New Street is 'King Charles House' (no. 29), now a restaurant. Originally built in 1577, these were the King's quarters during his occupation of the city. As dusk fell Parliamentary dragoons kicked down the front door as King Charles escaped from the rear entrance! As you walk down New Street and Friar Street you can still see surviving timber-framed houses that were in existence during the battle (as the medieval Greyfriars). During the evening of 3 September these streets would have been filled with troops engaged in bitter street fighting. The Scots used 'firepikes' to try to turn the cavalry attacks – these were leather jacks tied to the end of 16ft pikes and filled with burning tar that spat fire at the approaching horses. Turn right on to Pump Street and then on to High Street. The final Royalist counter-attack was probably along High Street as the King's English supporters mounted a last desperate charge to cover his escape as dragoons closed in on the royal quarters. The Guildhall, rebuilt in 1721–3, is on the site of the Town Hall, which was used as a prison after the battle and subsequently had to be fumigated. The Town Hall incorporated a law court, a prison and a large hall. Note the statues of Charles I and Charles II flanking the entrance to the Guildhall; above them is the head of a devil, pinned by his ears to the masonry. This is reputed to represent Cromwell who, legend has it, sold his soul to the devil in return for victory at Worcester! Pass down beside the Guildhall on Copenhagen Street and across Deansway and you will come to the quay side (Copenhagen Street car park). This is where many of the Scots made their last stand and finally surrendered, before then being herded into the Cathedral.

Further Reading

Ashley, M., *The English Civil War* (Stroud, 1990)

Atkin, M., *The Civil War in Worcestershire* (Stroud, 1995)

Atkin, M., *Cromwell's Crowning Mercy: the Battle of Worcester* (Stroud, 1998)

Atkin, M., *Worcestershire Under Arms* (Barnsley, 2004)

Carlton, C., *Going to the Wars* (London, 1992)

Fraser, A., *Cromwell: our chief of men* (London, 1975)

Fraser, A., *King Charles II* (London, 1979)

Gentles, I., *The New Model Army in England, Ireland and Scotland, 1645–1653* (Oxford, 1992)

Grainger, J.D., *Cromwell against the Scots: the last Anglo-Scottish war, 1650–1652* (East Linton, 1997)

Kenyon, J., *The Civil Wars of England* (London, 1996)

Morrill J., *The Impact of the English Civil War* (London, 1991)

Sherwood, R.E., *Civil War in the Midlands, 1642–1651* (Stroud, 1992)

Willis Bund, J.W., *The Civil War in Worcestershire 1642–1646 and the Scotch Invasion of 1651* (Birmingham, 1905)

Willis Bund, J.W., *The Battle of Worcester* (Worcester, 1908)

Notes

Preface

1 Hugh Peters, Chaplain to Oliver Cromwell, in a sermon preached to the army on 4 September 1651 (*Perfect Diurnall*, 6 September 1651).

Chapter One

1 R. Baxter, *Reliquae Baxterianae* (London, 1696), pt 1, p. 68.
2 See M. Atkin, *The Civil War in Worcestershire* (Stroud, 1995), pp. 34–7 for an account of the skirmish at Powick Bridge on 23 September 1642.
3 M. Atkin, *Worcestershire Under Arms* (Barnsley, 2004), pp. 30–60.
4 Common's Journal VI, p. 617.
5 *Mercurius Politicus*, 4–11 September 1651.
6 J. Washbourne, *Bibliotheca Gloucestrensis* (Gloucester, 1825), p. cxciv.
7 'Letter from a Scottish prisoner imprisoned in Chester after the battle', in J. Hughes (ed.), *Boscobel Tracts* (London, 1830), pp. 138–46.
8 Baxter, *Reliquae Baxterianae*, pt 1, p. 66.
9 Quoted in I. Gentles, *The New Model Army* (Oxford, 1992), p. 392.
10 Letter from Cromwell to his wife, 4 September 1650, in W.C. Abbott, *The Writings and Speeches of Oliver Cromwell* (Oxford, 1939), vol. II, p. 329.
11 Letter from Cromwell to the Council of State, 4 January 1651, in Abbott, *Writings and Speeches*, vol. II, p. 385.
12 Letter from Cromwell to William Lenthall, 4 August 1651, in M. Stace (ed.), *Cromwelliana* (London, 1810), p. 107.
13 Letter from Fleetwood at Banbury, 26 August 1651, in Stace (ed.), *Cromwelliana*, p. 110.
14 H. Cary, *Memorials of the Great Civil War in England from 1646 to 1652*, vol. 2 (London, 1842), p. 305.
15 Baxter, *Reliquae Baxterianae*, pt 1, p. 68.
16 B. Whitelocke, *Memorials of the English Affairs*, vol. III (1682 and Oxford, 1853), p. 503.
17 *Memoirs of the Life of Colonel Hutchinson, written by his wife Lucy* (London, 1889), p. 356.
18 F.S. Pearson, *Parish of Northfield Constables' Accounts 1620–1754* (Transcript, 1905–8), Birmingham Local Studies Collection S.A. 2, no. 269902, f.34a.
19 Letter from Lambert to Harrison, 5 August 1651, in Cary, *Memorials of the Great Civil War*, vol. 2, p. 295.
20 Letter of 7 August 1651 from Harrison to the Council of State.
21 Calendar of State Papers Domestic (hereafter CSPD), 16 December 1656, p. 197.

22 Earl of Clarendon, *The History of the Rebellion and Civil Wars in England*, ed. W. Dunn Macray (hereafter Clarendon), vol. 5, p. 178.

23 Washbourne, *Bibliotheca Gloucestrensis*, p. 434.

24 'Letter from a Scottish prisoner at Chester to France, 17 September 1651', in W. Matthews, *Charles II's Escape from Worcester* (London, 1967), pp. 29–30.

25 Calendar for the Committee for Compounding (hereafter *CCC*), 30 June 1652, p. 2588; CCC 4 February 1652, p. 2948.

26 Whitelocke, *Memorials*, p. 477.

27 Abbott, *Writings and Speeches*, vol. II, p. 449.

28 CSPD 10 March 1653, p. 207.

29 CSPD 26 August 1651, p. 373.

Chapter Two

 1 Letter from Robert Stapleton, 29 August 1651, in Cary, *Memorials of the Great Civil War*, vol. 2, p. 348.

 2 CSPD 31 March 1651, p. 120.

 3 Historic Manuscripts Commission (hereafter *HMC*) 12th Report, Appendix IX, p. 499.

 4 Pearson, *Northfield Constables' Accounts 1620–1754*, f.34a.

 5 HMC 12th Report, Appendix IX, p. 498.

 6 Letter to the Council of State, written from Gloucester, 23 August 1651, in Cary, *Memorials of the Great Civil War*, vol. 2, pp. 335–7.

 7 Pearson, *Northfield Constables' Accounts 1620–1754*, f.34a.

 8 Hughes (ed.), *Boscobel Tracts*, p. 140.

 9 Sir Nicholas Lechmere in HMC 5th Report, Appendix, p. 299.

10 WRO 850 Salwarpe, BA 1054/1.

11 *Mercurius Politicus*, 30 August 1651; Cary, *Memorials of the Great Civil War*, vol. 2, p. 348; Whitelocke, *Memorials*, p. 506.

12 Letter from Colonel Stapleton to Captain George Bishop, 29 August 1651, in Cary, *Memorials of the Great Civil War*, vol. 2, p. 348.

13 CSPD 17 September 1651, p. 437.

14 Atkin, *Civil War*, pp. 58–9; Whitelocke, *Memorials*, p. 506.

15 Leland, *Itinerary*, p. 71; J. Ogilby, *Britannia* (London, 1675).

16 H. Ellis, 'Letters from a Subaltern Officer in the Earl of Essex's army', *Archaeologia* XXXV (1853), 328.

17 Clarendon, vol. 5, p. 189.

18 Atkin, *Civil War*, pp. 105–16.

19 CSPD 27 August 1651, p. 376.

20 Pearson, *Northfield Constables' Accounts 1620–1754*, f.35.

21 CSPD 27 August 1651, p. 376.

22 Whitelocke, *Memorials*, p. 182.
23 Thomas Blount, *Boscobel* (1660), p. 8.
24 R.R. Temple, 'The Original Officer List of the New Model Army', *Bulletin of the Institute of Historical Research* 59 (1986).
25 D. Blackmore, *Arms and Armour of the English Civil Wars* (Royal Armouries, 1990), p. 68.
26 Sir John Smythe, *Observations and Orders Militarie* (London, 1595), pp. 25–6.
27 Washbourne, *Bibliotheca Gloucestrensis*, p. cxcv.
28 John Smythe, 'Certain Discourses Military', in J.R. Hale (ed.), *The Folger Shakespeare Library* (Cornell University Press, 1963), p. 71.
29 S. Reid, *Scots Armies of the 17th Century*, vol. 3 (1989), pp. 46–9.
30 Letter from Cromwell to the Speaker of the House of Commons, 4 September 1651, in Abbott, *Writings and Speeches*, vol. II, p. 462.
31 CSPD 9 September 1651, p. 419.
32 Robert Stapleton in *Perfect Diurnall*, 3 September 1651.
33 Richard Symonds, *Diary of the Marches of the Royal Army*.
34 Letter from a Royalist prisoner, in CSPD 17 September 1651, p. 436; Letter from Robert Stapleton, 29 August 1651, in Cary, *Memorials of the Great Civil War*, vol. 2, p. 348.
35 CSPD 1 September 1651, p. 395.

Chapter Three
1 Whitelocke, *Memorials*, p. 505.
2 Atkin, *Civil War*, pp. 112–13.
3 Blount, *Boscobel*, p. 15.
4 D. Miller, *Archaeological survey at Perry Wood, Worcester* (WHEAS Internal Report 1250, 2005), pp. 4–7.
5 Ottley Papers, vol. VIII, p. 247.
6 M. Atkin and W. Laughlin, *Gloucester and the Civil War: a city under siege* (Stroud, 1992), pp. 94–101.
7 *Ibbotson's Proceedings in Parliament*, p. 1560, quoted in V. Green, *History of Worcester* vol. I (1797), p. 280.
8 R. Wiseman, *Of Wounds, Of Gun-Shot Wounds, Of Fractures and Luxations* (1676, repr. Bath, 1977), p. 401.
9 Whitelocke, *Memorials*, p. 505.
10 Clarendon, vol. 5, p. 189.
11 Atkin, *Worcestershire Under Arms*, p. 49.
12 CSPD 2 September 1651, pp. 398–9.
13 The piles for the bridges were reputedly chopped up for firewood at the end of the nineteenth century: J.W. Willis Bund, *The Civil War in*

> *Worcestershire 1642–46 and the Scotch Invasion of 1651* (Birmingham, 1905), p. 260.
14 Clarendon, vol. 5, p. 190.

Chapter Four
1 Jeremiah 46:10.
2 D. Appleby, 'Essex Men at the Battle of Worcester', *English Civil War Times* 52 (1997), p. 27.
3 Letter from T. Scott and R. Salway to the Council of State, in Cary, *Memorials of the Great Civil War*, vol. 2, p. 364.
4 Sir James Turner, *Memoirs*, p. 62, quoted in C. Firth, *Cromwell's Army* (1992), p. 98.
5 CSPD 2 September 1651, pp. 398–9.
6 *A True and Faithful Narrative of Oliver Cromwell's Compact with the Devil for Seven Years . . . Related by Col. Lindsey* (1720).
7 Colonel Robert Stapleton in *Perfect Diurnall*, 3 September 1651.
8 Clarendon, vol. 5, p. 192.
9 WRO Lechmere Diary.
10 WRO 899:31 BA3669/2 (v).
11 Letter from Cromwell to William Lenthall, 3 September 1651, in Abbott, *Writings and Speeches*, vol. II, p. 461.
12 Willis Bund, *The Civil War in Worcestershire*, p. 254.

Chapter Five
1 Robert Stapleton in *Perfect Diurnall*, 3 September 1651.
2 Wiseman, *Of Wounds*, p. 420.
3 E. Ludlow, *Memoirs*, vol. I, p. 281.
4 'Letter from Oliver Cromwell to the Speaker of the House of Commons, 3 September 1651', in Stace (ed.), *Cromwelliana*, p. 110; WRO 899:31 BA3669/2 (v).
5 The features referred to on modern maps as 'Cromwell's Entrenchments' are not military works and a recent study has concluded that they are the scars left by former quarrying. See D. Miller, *Archaeological survey at Perry Wood*, pp. 4–7.
6 'Letter from T. Scott and R. Salway to the Council of State', in Cary, *Memorials of the Great Civil War*, vol. 2, p. 363.
7 Letter from Hamilton to his wife, Commandery Museum, Worcester.
8 Cary, *Memorials of the Great Civil War*, vol. 2, p. 363.
9 HMC 10th Report, Appendix VI, p. 175.
10 Wiseman, *Of Wounds*, p. 441.
11 'Letter from Oliver Cromwell to the Speaker of the House of Commons, 3 September 1651', in Stace (ed), *Cromwelliana*, p. 110.

12 Blount, *Boscobel*, p. 14.
13 'Letter from T. Scott and R. Salway to the Council of State', in Cary, *Memorials of the Great Civil War*, vol. 2, p. 354.
14 'When we took the fort, we turned his own guns upon him': Cromwell in Letter of 2 September to the Speaker of the House of Commons, in Abbott, *Writings and Speeches*, vol. II, p. 461.
15 'An Exact Narrative and Relation (1660)', in Matthews, *Charles II's Escape*, p. 86; *Perfect Diurnall*, 1–8 September 1651, reprinted in Stace (ed.), *Cromwelliana*, pp. 112–13, and Atkin, *Civil War*, p. 168.
16 Letter of a Scottish prisoner, in Hughes (ed.), *Boscobel Tracts*, p. 143.
17 Blount, *Boscobel*, p. 15.
18 Letter of a Scottish prisoner, in Hughes (ed.), *Boscobel Tracts*, p. 144; *Relation of the defeat of the King's army at Worcester, 3 September 1651*, in CSPD 17 September 1651, p. 437.
19 HMC 10th Report, Appendix VI, p. 175.
20 Blount, *Boscobel*, p. 15.
21 M. Atkin, *Cromwell's Crowning Mercy: the Battle of Worcester, 1651* (Stroud, 1998), pp. 165–7.
22 CSPD 1 November 1651, p. 2.
23 Cary, *Memorials of the Great Civil War*, vol. II, p. 364.
24 Letters from Cromwell to Lenthall, 3 September 1651, in Abbott, *Writings and Speeches*, vol. II, pp. 461–2.
25 HMC 10th Report, Appendix VI, p. 175.
26 Letter from Cromwell to Lenthall, 8 September 1651, in Abbott, *Writings and Speeches*, vol. II, p. 467.
27 WRO Audit of the City Accounts, 1640–69.
28 D. Stevenson, *King or Covenant? Voices from the Civil War* (East Lothian, 1996), p. 124; *Dictionary of National Biography*, vol. XX, p. 48.
29 HMC 10th Report, Appendix 6, p. 175.
30 Letter of 6 September from Harrison, cited in Willis Bund, *The Civil War in Worcestershire*, p. 251; Whitelocke, *Memorials*, p. 508.
31 St Michael Bedwardine, Churchwardens' Accounts 1651–2, ff.111, 112, 113d.
32 C. Beardsmore, 'City Walls Road: summary report of the archaeology', *Worcestershire Archaeology Newsletter* 17 (1976), p. 21.
33 Letter from Cromwell to the Speaker of the House of Commons, 4 September 1651, in Abbott, *Writings and Speeches*, vol. II, p. 463.
34 *Perfect Diurnall*, 6 September 1651.

Chapter Six

1 Letter of Scottish officer, in CSPD 17 September 1651, p. 437
2 Whitelocke, *Memorials*, p. 348; WRO Audit of the City Accounts, 1640–69.

3 Wiseman, *Of Wounds*, p. 441.
4 Baxter, *Reliquae Baxterianae*, pt 1, p. 67.
5 *Ibid.*
6 *Mercurius Politicus*, 4–11 September 1651.
7 *Memoirs of Captain John Hodgson* (Pontefract, 1994), p. 30; CSPD 8 October 1651, p. 470.
8 Pearson, *Northfield Constables' Accounts 1620–1754*, ff.34a–36.
9 Clarendon, vol. 5, p. 191.
10 Whitelocke, *Memorials*, p. 508; *Mercurius Politicus*, 4–11 September 1651.
11 Pearson, *Northfield Constables' Accounts 1620–1754*, f.36.
12 Letter in CSPD 17 September 1651, p. 437.
13 CSPD 1651, p. 449; Letter from Cromwell to Cotton, 2 October 1651, in Abbott, *Writings and Speeches*, vol. II, p. 482.
14 *Memoirs of Lady Fanshawe* (1830), pp. 113–17.
15 BM Add. Ms 31955, transcript of Pepys Ms 2141: copy in WRO 899.31. Whitgreave describes possibly the same men coming to the door asking for provisions and dressings for their wounds: A. Fea, *After Worcester Fight* (London, 1904), Tract III, p. 165.
16 Whitelocke, *Memorials*, p. 516.
17 Pearson *Northfield Constables' Accounts 1620–1754*, f.34a.
18 CSPD 17 December 1651, p. 67.
19 Whitelocke, *Memorials*, p. 512.
20 CSPD 1 September 1654, p. 353.
21 CSPD 2 December 1651, p. 44.
22 CSPD 21 October 1651, p. 363.
23 Whitelocke, *Memorials*, p. 510.
24 CSPD 17 October 1651, p. 480.
25 C. Boyer (ed.), *Ships Passenger Lists, National and New England: 1600–1825* (California, 1977), p. 154.
26 Boyer (ed.), *Ships Passenger Lists*, p. 161.
27 'Letters written by Mr Moray . . . from Ware River in Montjack Bay, Virginia, Feb. 1 1665', *William and Mary Quarterly* (July 1922), 2nd ser. no. 3, p. 160.
28 Lord Braybrooke (ed.), *Diary of Samuel Pepys*, vol. 1 (Everyman, 1906), p. 408.
29 Some of the correspondence of this company was published in S. Wells, *A History of the drainage of the Great Level of the Fens called Bedford Level* (London, 1830), vol. 1. Hereafter Wells 1830.
30 Wells, 1830, pp. 229–31: 666 yards of white kersey were ordered to make up the smocks, at a price not to exceed 2*s* 3*d* per yard.
31 Wells, 1830, p. 241 (for 24 December 1651): a hassack was a turf cut, moulded and dried for fuel.

32 T. Craddock, *History of Wisbech and the Fens* (Wisbech, 1849), pp. 147–8.
33 CSPD 17 December 1651, p. 67; CSPD 2 August 1652, p. 353.
34 CSPD 22 January 1656, p. 126.
35 *Pers. comm.* Erica Enslin-Franklin.

Chapter Seven
1 Hughes (ed.), *Boscobel Tracts*, p. 285. Hereafter Blount, *Boscobel*.
2 Fea, *After Worcester Fight*, Tract 1, pp. 5–44.
3 Boscobel Tract, pp. 183–287.
4 The King's account of his escape (1680) in Matthews, *Charles II's Escape*, p. 38.
5 Fea, *After Worcester Fight*, Tract 1, p. 6.
6 Blount, *Boscobel*, p. 229.
7 A. Fea, *The Flight of the King* (London, 1904), Tract II (Boscobel), p. 99.
8 Blount, *Boscobel*, p. 237.
9 Fea, *After Worcester Fight*, Tract 1, p. 29.
10 Fea, *Flight*, Tract III, p. 166.
11 J.F. Downes, quoted in A. Fraser, *King Charles II* (London, 1979), p. 122 note.
12 *Letter Book*, Rawlinson MSS.
13 Fea, *Flight*, Tract IV, p. 190.
14 R. Ollard, *The Escape of Charles II* (London, 1986), p. 95.
15 Blount, *Boscobel*, p. 269.
16 Fea, *Flight*, Tract IV, pp. 227, 200.
17 Alford Deposition in Matthews, *Charles II's Escape*, p. 128.
18 Blount, *Boscobel*, p. 276.
19 Blount, *Boscobel*, p. 279.
20 Calendar State Papers Venetian, vol. 28 (1647–52), p. 202.
21 CSPD 1 November 1651, p. 2.

INDEX